# AUTOBIOGRAPHY
## OF A
## ONE YEAR OLD

D0522596

First published in Great Britain in 2000
This paperback edition published 2001

13 15 17 19 20 18 16 14

First published by
Ebury Press
Random House
20 Vauxhall Bridge Road
London SW1 2SA

www.randomhouse.co.uk

Random House Australia (Pty) Limited
20 Alfred Street, Milsons Point, Sydney,
New South Wales 2061, Australia

Random House New Zealand Limited
18 Poland Road, Glenfield, Auckland 10,
New Zealand

Random House South Africa (Pty) Limited
Endulini, 5A Jubilee Road, Parktown 2193,
South Africa

Random House UK Limited Reg. No. 954009

A CIP catalogue record for this book is available from the British Library

ISBN 9780091880699

Papers used by Ebury Press are natural, recyclable products made
from wood grown in sustainable forests.

Designed by Anthony Cohen
Illustrations by Sally Artz
Printed and bound in Great Britain by
Cox & Wyman Ltd, Reading, Berkshire

# AUTOBIOGRAPHY
## OF A
## ONE YEAR OLD

Rohan Candappa

EBURY
PRESS

For Jan, without whom I would never have
become a writer.
And for Pickle, without whom I would never have
become this writer.
Thank you.

'The childhood shews the man,
As morning shews the day. Be famous then
By wisdom; as thy Empire must extend,
So let extend thy mind o'er all the World.'

Milton, *Paradise Regained*



'Big Huuuggg!'

Tinky-Winky, Dipsy, La-La
& Po — The Teletubbies

# INTRODUCTION

**H**ave you noticed how people writing their autobiographies are getting younger and younger? Appalling, isn't it? What on earth can they have to write about?

My book is, of course, entirely different. I've got loads to write about. I am endeavouring to convey the sheer life-affirming voluptuousness of those heady months between the ages of one and two, when new experiences and startling revelations await the forming mind at every turn.

I'll also be writing a fair bit about poo. Yes, poo looms large in what is to follow, so if you're at all squeamish, it's probably best to check out now and select a less messy tome. (I hear the new Hannibal Lecter book is very good.)

However, if you do stick with it, you're in for one hell of a ride. That's because I've had a cracking year. As to why I didn't start my memoir from the day I was born, all I can say is that it's a question of vanity. If I were to recount the story of those early days, I wouldn't come out of it too well. For a start, I looked like Winston Churchill. Also, I seemed to spend most of the year asleep. Or crying. And when I wasn't doing either of these, it was more a case of stuff being done to me, than me doing the actual doing. Who wants to be remembered like that?

Then on my first birthday I started to crawl.

Talk about liberation. The world was my oyster. The only way to convey the joy of this new found mobility is to recourse to analogy. Remember what it was like when you got your first car? How free you felt? How ready to take on the world? How grown up? The first crawl is pretty much the same. Only better. Because you don't have to fork out for petrol, tax or insurance and the brand-new, top-of-the-range model you're in charge of actually improves the older it gets.

As to how I have structured the book, a month by month approach seemed the most logical arrangement. That said, the strict chronological order of events may get jumbled sometimes. But hopefully it will make sense. You may also detect a certain maturing in my outlook and increasing sophistication in my thinking as time goes by. Whether this maturing process actually happened, or whether I imposed it on the morass of events that comprise my memories in order to make me look better, I'll leave up to you to decide.

However, before we get to the meat of my month by month sojourn, I'd like to share the following with you. It is my first attempt at the journal I started in order to write this book.

## My First Journal

**Day One.** Got up, played, cried, milk, porridge, pooed, cried, played, napped, pooed, cried, played, ate, pooed, cried, bathed, played, milk, bed.

**Day Two.** Got up, played, cried, milk, porridge, pooed, cried, played, napped, pooed, cried, played, ate, pooed, cried, bathed, played, milk, bed.

**Day Three.** Got up, played, cried, milk, porridge, didn't poo, cried louder than normal, played unenthusiastically, still didn't poo, cried in a manner that revisited the earlier crying but invested in it a hidden subtext of a deeper, almost spiritual, unhappiness, refused to play, managed a few mouthfuls, poooooooooooed big style, cried in a mixture of happiness and relief, milk, bed.

I realised that if I carried on writing in that fashion, my chances of being nominated for the Nobel Prize for Literature, let alone winning it, would be slim, exceedingly slim. So I stopped and regrouped. And had a bit of a ponder.

I contemplatively sucked on a rusk, using the physical activity and the sugar rush to aid my concentration. As that brittle biscuit dissolved satisfyingly in my mouth, the realisation dawned that insight lies not in the simple recounting of experiences but in the collision of experience with opinion. That what I should write was not really a continuous story, more a series of dispatches from the front line. And that if I followed this approach, and trusted in the intelligence of the reader, then they would be able to discern the big picture without me having to spell it out for them.

I must admit, it was an approach that appealed to me. After all, why should I do all the work?

# MONTH
# XIII

In which, if you believe the books, I should be able to
get in to a standing position, clap hands and indicate wants
in ways other than crying.
Yeah, right.

# Parents.
# A Few Thoughts On The Thorny Subject Of

E ssentially parents are odd fish. Their ways are
mysterious and many of their ideas are just plain
bizarre. I'm not sure what the point of them is
but, like junk mail or a sniffle in winter, they are
exceedingly hard to avoid; parents come with the territory.
Standard issue is two, though one is fairly common, and
three or four not unknown. I, myself, have in my employ
two parents of the usual variety.

If you, like me, have a duo of parents they normally fall
into two distinct categories. The first category is Smooth,
the second is Hairy. Smooths tend to be full-time staff
whereas Hairies are, at best, part-timers. Some people I've
met claim their Hairies do equal if not more hours than
their Smooths, but frankly I find that a little hard to believe.
Smooths also tend to handle more of the refuelling
functions and the nether region work.

Now, because I spend more of my time with Smooth,
the appearance of Hairy, when it occurs, is a situation
that can be exploited in many ways. Prime among these is
the ruse of spending most of the day in dispute with
Smooth, then being all smiles and cuddles when Hairy
turns up. It's a divide-and-rule ploy that never fails to
produce results. I know it sounds a little devious, but it's
one of the few chances you have of out-manoeuvring

parents who so often hold the upper hand.

And that is the nub of the parent conundrum.

You see, although the parents are undoubtedly working for me, by some ludicrous twist of fate, they have been put in charge. It is a position they are so patently ill equipped to handle that it leaves you with the disquieting feeling that you are the victim of some monstrous mistake. I mean, they know so little about me and the world I inhabit that it's hardly surprising so many of the decisions they make about me are completely wrong.

For instance, no one likes porridge. Absolutely no one. That's why, given a choice, at breakfast people eat cereal, or toast, or croissant, or pancakes, or bacon and egg. So how come I'm force-fed porridge every morning?

Or what about the things they put in my cot? Some nights I get in and it's like trying to find a seat in an over-crowded rail carriage. Okay, I admit that by now I know some of the chaps who share my cot, but honestly I'm really only on nodding terms with most of them. For heaven's sake I'm trying to sleep in here, don't I deserve a little space of my own?

The bitter truth is that parents are in charge. So, one way or another, you have to discover your own way of getting along with them.

The spectrum of possible strategies you can employ ranges from total deference, through collaboration, to outright war. My advice is, don't put all your toys in one toy box. Vary your approach. It'll keep you interested and them on their toes. Just because they're in charge doesn't mean you can't be in control.

# What's In A Name?

They say the Eskimos have hundreds of words for types of snow. Pathetic.

I've loads more than that for types of poo. When the stuff features as such a big part in your life you tend to dwell on the subject. And, all too often you don't just dwell on the subject, you frequently dwell in it as well. There is something deeply deflating about having to sit in your own poo. Let's just say it is not the biggest boost to one's self esteem. So of course I scream my head off. Wouldn't you?

Back to the naming of the names. I won't detain you with the full list, but just pass on some of my own particular favourites. Top of the Pops is grouty poo. This is the type of poo that gets into all manner of cracks and crevices, makes itself comfortable, then dries. On first encounter, grouty poo looks inoffensive. And it is dry, which makes it less gooey to handle. However, the downside is that grouty poo dries rock hard. To get rid of the stuff you almost have to resort to a chisel.

To trump the challenge of ordinary grouty poo (or OGP as I sometimes abbreviate it) is the horror that is overnight grouty poo (ONGP). This doesn't so much dry, as set. Like concrete. Forget the chisel. For ONGP you need a fat labourer sporting low-slung jeans, wielding a pneumatic drill. That's the only way to shift it.

Next up is pollocky poo. This is poo that splatters across

pristine white surfaces in a random, abstract fashion. It is poo that in many ways crosses the boundaries of poo itself. Is it really poo? Why is there no form or shape to it? Isn't it really just a mess? What does it mean? My personal belief is that pollocky poo is poo, and that it is great poo. But it is poo that obeys the rules of its own aesthetic. The trick is to accept it on its own terms.

Then there is BTP. BTP is relatively rare and can vary tremendously in shape, size and consistency. What makes it special is not so much its nature but the reaction it can engender in parents. BTP can turn the most laid back of individuals into a veritable maelstrom of activity. If you want to see what a tornado looks like close up, just indulge in a little BTP. That's bath tub poo.

Finally, of course, there's chewy poo. But maybe we shouldn't go into that right now. After all, you might be eating.

# Nursery Crimes One. Circulating Teddy Bears

'Round and round the garden
Like a teddy bear.
One step, two steps
Tickly under there'

Point of order Mr Chairman?

I have spent considerable time in many gardens and I have
as yet to find a single instance of teddy bears going round
them. I have also consulted with numerous of my colleagues
who, between them, have access to many other gardens and
they confirm that they can recall no occasion on which a
teddy bear has gone round a garden.

Frankly, the whole teddy-bear-round-the-garden thing is
little more than a blatant, spurious, and all too often,
successful incantation designed to distract an individual
prior to a totally unprovoked tickling attack.

It is a con and a trap.

In the light of this transparent misuse of power I have
decided to pay particular attention to all
nursery rhymes that I encounter from here
on. I mean, if parents can do it once, what's
to stop them doing it again?

I shall report back as and when
necessary.

# You Need Hands

On the whole a damn good idea. Hands are, so far, the most useful bit of me that I have discovered. You can pick things up with them. You can drop things with them. You can fling things with them. You can hit things with them. You can scratch and hit parents with them. You can get them caught in doors. And drawers. And small spaces. Because hands are located on the ends of arms (a very fine arrangement), you can reach up with them and pull things down. Plus, my own personal favourite, you can wave them about for no particular reason.

Hands are also useful for getting about with. Crawling would be a lot trickier if you didn't have hands. Or, if they were positioned anywhere other than on the ends of your arms. Obviously a lot of thinking has gone into the working of hands; to whoever was responsible, I would like to extend my most sincere thanks.

However, I must admit it was a moment of some perplexity when I realised (way back in my first year of being) that the hands that followed me around were actually attached to me. The insight that these little chaps were under my control was a revelation. Although, in the beginning, it is probably more accurate to say my hands were 'under my influence'. I'd want them to grab a ball. The hands would go for the ball, then, at the last moment, knock it away. I'd want them to pick up a twig from the ground and put it in my mouth; the hands would decide to poke me in the eye with it instead. I would want them to stroke Smooth's face in a way that conveyed love, respect and admiration but they would whack into her with a gouging ferocity that almost scarred her for life.

So early on my hands were, excuse the pun, a bit of a handful.

My control over them extended to little more than suggesting things they might like to get involved with. Much as you might suggest to a recalcitrant puppy that it might like to get off your head now, I would suggest to my hands that they might like putting the Marmite soldier in my mouth. Then all I could do was sit back and see if my hands would take up the suggestion. Yes, it was frustrating. Yes, I did end up with a lot of Marmite in my hair, over my cheeks, and on one memorable occasion between my toes. (OK, I'll admit that I was trying to see if I could get my whole foot in my mouth.)

What I discovered was that over time the hands became much more amenable to suggestions. I suppose I was getting the hang of them. Or maybe they were just resigning themselves to the fact that they were stuck with me so we might as well get on and work on things together.

Now, if there are any youngsters out there reading this who are finding that they are having a torrid time with their own hands and are considering chucking it all in and trying to start doing things with their feet instead, I'd just say, don't. Stick with your hands. Persevere. It gets more accurate. And it gets more fun. You can do it. I know you can. Even though I'm quite good with my hands now, I'm humble enough to know that I've still got a lot to learn. Frankly I can't wait. The other day I spotted Hairy using his hands to pull things out of the wall, just where it meets the floor, and uncovering three little holes. I'm not sure, but I've got a pretty good idea that if I can get those things out of the wall myself when no one's looking, then those three holes are just about the right size for me to get my fingers into. Wouldn't that be great?

# A Full And Frank Explanation
# As To Why I Sometimes Blow Snot Bubbles
# With My Nose

**Because I can.**

# Pause And Effect

Picture the scene. I'm trundling along, minding my own business, trying to remember the names of all Seven Dwarfs, when Hairy opens a cupboard straight onto my head. The pain is unbelievable. But before my face crumples like a rapidly deflating inflatable paddling pool, before I let rip a wail that bemoans the fundamental unfairness of the world we live in, I pause.

Why?

To the uninitiated, it probably appears that the sudden intrusion of excruciating pain has come as such a shock that, for a moment, I am totally at a loss. When I work out that I'm in pain, and the appropriate response to pain is noise, I open up the throttle on both lungs. However, one fact should throw a little doubt on such a simplistic analysis. The pause only happens when someone is watching. If I'm on my own, then I'm screaming the instant I feel the pain.

The shark in *Jaws* was more frightening because of the music that preceded it. The lift-off of an Apollo rocket was more exciting because of the countdown. And my howl of pain is more searing because of the split second of silence that precedes it. Why? Well, it's because for the watching parent there is no appropriate response to that split second. That moment has the ability to isolate the parent. And render them useless. That moment has true power. And that's why I pause.

For effect.

# The Stalker

At what age does paranoia set in? At what age do we start to think there's someone out to get us? Someone watching everything we do? Someone going wherever we go? I have no idea what happened in your case, but with me I'm not even two years old and I'm being stalked. If I'm in my room, The Stalker's there. When I go downstairs, The Stalker's there. If I go out to visit friends, The Stalker's there too. Even when I'm ensconced in my buggy, being pushed down to the shops, I just have to look across at the shop windows and The Stalker's there as well.

Why?

What have I done? What does The Stalker want? Who sent him? Most disquieting of all, why do I find The Stalker so damned attractive?

# Sticks And Stones May Break My Bones But Honestly They Taste Better Than The Goo I Get Fed Most Of The Time

W hy do I put things I find on the ground in my mouth? I know there's a theory that says I'm not actually trying to eat the things but merely trying to feel them on account of the fact that the nerves in the mouth develop faster than the nerves in, for example, my fingers. Well, wrong! I am trying to eat the things. Because on the whole they taste better than the 'Give us this day our daily goo' that gets sludged towards me at regular intervals. And not only goo, but tepid and occasionally ice-cold goo.

As for the colour of the goos in question, please don't get me started. Do the parents not even have a basic grasp on presentation? Apparently not. Today's menu, for instance, was tepid taupe goo to start, with chilled beige goo to follow, rounded off with crunchy woodchip-style rusk as the pièce de résistance. You want to know why we go for rusks in such a big way? They may not taste of anything, but at least you can feel the damn things in your mouth. Hence our endless foraging for something to eat.

But why do we insist on picking things up off the floor to eat?

Come on. Think about it. It's all we can reach.

# The Game

I love it. I love it. I love it. The buzz you get after you've played well is incredible. It leaves you with such an overwhelming feeling of joy. And achievement. And power. You feel like anything is possible. You crawl just a little bit taller after you've got a particularly high score.

I've often tried to analyse just what it is about the Game that makes it such a glorious, addictive pursuit. All I can come up with is that it combines absolute physicality with complex strategy. Even a master tactician like Sun Tzu would drop his chopsticks, leap to his feet and start to applaud. And you have to out-think and out-manoeuvre an opponent who starts off not only in a superior position, but possesses all the aces in terms of size and sheer physical strength (some might say brute force).Why no one has snapped up the rights to televise the Game is beyond me.

You do, admittedly, have one advantage. You are able to decide whether to play the Game or not. But the advantage is short-lived. Once you execute your opening gambit, your opponent is alerted to the fact that the Game's afoot and they're all over you like porridge on a sleepy suit. Hence the importance of scoring as many points as possible with that opening play. Also the importance of not playing the Game too often. The value of surprise cannot be overemphasised.

As to the venue for the Game, my own particularly Wembley is my high chair. It's where I first played the Game. It's where I know the layout. It's where I know the angles.

But let's get down to the basics. Like all the finest sports, the aim of the Game is very simple: to get as much food as possible on the clothes and the person of whoever is trying to feed you. Your opponent, the person feeding you, tries to stay as free from foodstuffs as they can. And that's it.

It's a classic confrontation of two individuals. It's a battle of strength, skill, tactics and wills. It's Ali versus Frazier, it's Sampras versus Agassi. It's you versus your parent.

The scoring system goes like this:

| | |
|---|---|
| **A gloop on feeder's hand** | **4 points.** |
| **On feeder's arm** | **8 points** |
| **On feeder's leg** | **9 points** |
| **On feeder's torso** | **12 points** |
| **On feeder's face** | **23 points** |
| **In feeder's hair** | **32 points** |
| **In feeder's eye** | **51 points** |

Then, of course, the scores have to be adjusted according to the Universal Clothing Weighting System (UCWS):

- **Feeder in pyjamas/night attire:** Multiply score by factor of 1.
- **Feeder dressed in lounging about aimlessly attire:** Multiply score by factor of 1.5.
- **Feeder dressed smart/casual:** Multiply score by factor of 2.
- **Feeder dressed for work:** Multiply score by factor of 3. (*Bonus accrues in this and subsequent category, if parent's tie is hit: extra 20 points.*)
- **Feeder dressed for important work meeting:** Multiply score by factor of 3.5.
- **Feeder dressed for extremely rare evening out:** Multiply score by factor of 5.

Two Fabric Bonuses worth noting are:

**Gloop on silk:** Add 50 to unadjusted score.

**Gloop on cashmere:** Add 62 to unadjusted score.

Your basic moves are pretty straightforward:

| | |
|---|---|
| | The left-hand upswing |
| | The left-hand downswing |
| | The right-hand upswing |
| | The right-hand downswing |
| | The double-handed smash, both up and down |
| | The sideswipe left to right, and right to left |

Then there are combinations that aim to outfox the opponent by linking two or more of the basic moves. There are also numerous techniques using the mouth and lips: the dribble, the blow, the headshake, the puke, the choke and cough, the fake-choke and cough coupled with the blow, and the rather sneaky fake-kiss and blow.

Finally, of course, there is the master move. The hole-in-one, the home run. Namely, The Bowl Grab And Fling. It's a stonker. Get it right and you're home and dry. Which is more than can be said for the feeder. Don't get me wrong, it is one of the most difficult and riskiest moves to try, but the results can be spectacular. Get it right and the word soon spreads. The next time you crawl into the sandpit, heads turn, paths are cleared, rusks are proffered. Get it right, and the look of sheer horror on the feeder's face is a joy to behold. You know you've won. They know you've won. More importantly, they know you know you've won.

But a word of warning, they're crap losers. Boy do they make you suffer. But it doesn't matter, because you've won.

God, I love the Game. Love it, love it, love it.

# MONTH
# XIV

In which I should be able to wave bye-bye, stand alone
and bend over and pick up an object.
I can't wait.

# Who Will Rid Me Of This Troublesome Dark?

**D**ark. I'm not entirely sure that I've got a handle on it. Dark mainly turns up when you're tired. It kind of lurks about, in the corners of places, biding its time. Then the very second your eyelids droop, dark's in like a shot. If you don't want dark to take over you have to act fast. Force those eyelids open. Because the second dark sees you opening your eyes it tends to back off.

But even though it's backed off, it hasn't gone far. It tends to sneak away and hide. Dark loves being under things. The other day I found loads of the stuff under the cot. That night when I went to bed, it was still there. I've also noticed that dark hides behind curtains. So when, of an evening, Hairy or Smooth pulls the curtains together dark floods out and starts to fill the room. Then, in the morning, when they open the curtains, dark rushes back to hide in the folds.

Dark hates certain switches. If you can get your hands on any of these switches you've pretty much got dark on the run. Unfortunately these switches, as well as being at a stupid height, appear to be the parents' own personal playthings. If they ever spot you near one of these switches, you're soon whisked away.

Now we come to the thorny issue of whether or not I'm afraid of the dark. It may appear to the less astute observer, on account of my regular wailing when dark turns up, that I am, indeed, afraid of the dark. For the record, I must state unequivocally that this is not the case. I wail because of the limitations the dark puts upon me. It's quite hard to see things in the dark. And because it's quite hard to see things, it's quite hard to do things. And that's what upsets me. It's not the possibility of what might happen to me in the dark, but the impossibility of the things I can't do on account of the fact that I can't see what the hell's going on.

It's all about lost opportunities. Don't tell me you haven't ever cried over a lost opportunity. Life is short and I've no time to waste. There are sandpits to conquer, shelves to pull down, books to shred and rusks to chew up and drop all over the house. So I've no time for this dark malarkey. I'm a very busy baby.

# Sorted

**S**orting shapes. What's all that about? What possible use could it be to you in later life? Granted, it's a milestone at the time. A real sense of accomplishment. General rejoicing all round. The respect of your peers. Parental approval. But absolutely no use when you get out into the real world, unless you become a postman in a universe where letter boxes come in unusual shapes, and everyone sends each other hat boxes and exceedingly large Toblerones. How likely is that?

The basic principle seems fairly straightforward. On the one hand you have shapes, on the other hand you have holes. The idea is to fit the shapes through the holes. Sometimes the shapes want to go through the holes. Sometimes the shapes don't want to go through the holes. Or maybe it's the holes that don't want the shapes to go through them. Perhaps the holes, like the latest club, operate some kind of arbitrary door policy.

Being an egalitarian individual, I decided that such a policy was deeply divisive. Who gave the holes the right to decide who should or shouldn't be let in? That's why I spent many a long hour trying to get any shape to fit through any hole. It was a thankless task, but one that I eagerly undertook in the pursuit of a more just society. But my efforts were all in vain. Some holes would not allow certain shapes in no matter how forcefully I tried to break down their innate prejudices. And, I regret to have to inform you,

Hairy and Smooth looked on in disappointment at my attempts to create a fairer world by pushing what was, in their outmoded, conservative view, the wrong shape through the wrong hole.

Then I finally gained insight into what the sorting shapes thing was all about. It was all about fitting in. Knowing your place. It was a parental attempt to impress upon me, as an individual, that unless I discovered where I belonged and fitted in, then my life ahead would be one filled with frustration and failure. The sorting shapes thing wasn't about sorting shapes, it was about maintaining the status quo. That's why the parents attached such importance to it.

# Nursery Crimes Two. When The Wind Blows

'Rock-a-bye Baby
On the treetop.
When the wind blows
The cradle will rock.
When the bough breaks
The cradle will fall
Down will come baby, cradle and all.'

Point one: what on earth is the cradle doing in the tree in the first place?

What kind of psycho parent is going to lovingly nestle a baby in a cradle, then clamber up a tree with it and leave it there? And, note, not just anywhere in the tree, but right up to the treetop?

Point two: when the cradle is in the treetop, what starts happening?

The wind starts blowing. You might think that even the cruellest parent would feel just a tad remorseful and climb back up the tree and rescue said baby. But no. Oh no. Quite the opposite. The parent self-evidently just sits it out and waits for things to go from bad to badder.

How do I know this?

Well, just examine what happens next. What happens next is that the bough breaks. Now, I know for a fact that a wind has to be pretty damn powerful to break a bough, especially a bough that is strong enough to have carried the weight of a cradle and a baby in the first place. So we are confronted by the nightmare scenario, 'Down will come baby, cradle and all'.

And that, my friends, is the end of the nursery rhyme.

There is no mention of the parent rushing to the base of the tree in an effort to catch the plummeting baby. I mean, I don't think I'd mind if the parent missed the catch, but not even to have tried is, in my book, an outrage.

But now here's the really sick part of the whole deal. This nightmare tale of deliberate cruelty, staggering evil and trauma-inducing indifference to child welfare isn't a searing indictment of the contemporary world, designed to make us agitate for change and alert us to the dangers of inadequate child-rearing in a society whose values have gone seriously awry. Oh no. This nightmare is supposed to help us go to sleep.

I ask you, what kind of sick individual came up with that toss of the dice?

# Entertaining The Parents

I'll tell you another thing about my parents. They get bored very easily. So it falls upon me to entertain and amuse them. Often the most innocuous, banal pastimes will get them grinning like idiots. Take today for instance. I found a sleepy suit discarded on the floor (I really must tidy up more often ) and I was trying to do up the poppers on it. I'd seen Hairy and Smooth do it loads of times and if they could do it, well it couldn't be that difficult. So I thought I'd have a go.

Anyway, there I was, merrily minding my own business, doing my own thing, when Smooth spotted me. Good grief, the way she reacted you would think I'd just built a scale model of the Eiffel Tower out of baby breadsticks. She was grinning all the way from here to somewhere a long way off. And get this, she even went and got Hairy in from another room to watch too.

To tell the truth by this time I was kind of bored with what I was doing, I mean the poppers weren't really popping like they should. So I was of a mind to stop and do something else. But then I looked up at Smooth and Hairy. And they were just so happy. So I couldn't stop, could I? I had to keep on doing it for ages. The things you have to do to keep your parents amused.

# Playing Peepo

**C**omplex it isn't.

● **Rule One:** Hide behind something or lift something in front of eyes.
● **Rule Two:** Pop out from whatever you are hiding behind or lower whatever you're holding in front of your eyes.
● **Rule Three:** Whoever you are playing with shouts 'Peepo'.

And that's it.

Yes, I know it's hardly going to make it as an Olympic sport, but it has a certain simple charm and the parents love it. Boy, do they love it. They are absolutely hooked on it. Once they start playing you might as well write off the rest of the day. I mean, what is the attraction?

Play 'Peepo' for any length of time with your parents and the inevitable thought comes to you that these people are, how can I put it, a few teddy bears short of a picnic.

# The Stalker. It Gets Worse

Still can't shake The Stalker off. There really should be a law. Knowing that everywhere you go there is someone watching you can be a tad disquieting. Mid-poo is not a moment when you really want to look up and catch sight of someone staring directly at you.

Mind you, it does boost the ego when you ponder the fact that someone out there thinks you're worthy of this kind of attention. Having a Stalker is a reflection of the fact that I have achieved a certain level of celebrity. And as long as The Stalker doesn't actively try to interfere with what I'm doing, should it really bother me?

On another level it strikes me that The Stalker doesn't really seem to have a life of their own. The Stalker is, apparently, happy to live vicariously through me. Sad.

So I decided to confront The Stalker and say something along the lines of 'much as I am flattered by your attentions, and much as I generally agree with Socrates' maxim that an unexamined life is not worth living, maybe an over-examined life can be pretty unbearable too, and haven't you got anything better to do anyway?'

At which point I noticed a facet of the situation that completely freaked me out.

The Stalker copies everything I do. I open my mouth, The Stalker opens their mouth. I raise my arm, The Stalker raises their arm. I crawl towards The Stalker, The Stalker crawls towards me. What's worse is that The Stalker is wearing exactly the same thing that I'm wearing. And – here's the detail that finally alerted me to the fact that I was dealing with a complete fruit-cake – The Stalker had even replicated the porridge mark I'd got on my sleeve that morning!

This was just too weird. I crawled screaming from the room. I reached the sanctuary of the next room. Where The Stalker was already waiting for me.

Would this horror never end?

# A Short Meditation On Plastic, Often Pondered As I Play With A Plethora Of Toys

**Doesn't it come in neutral colours?**

# Sandpit Etiquette. A Few Pointers
# For The Novice

The sandpit is not an unstructured environment. Behind the seemingly anarchic free-for-all, hierarchies and lowerarchies are formed, dissolved and formed again in a constantly shifting kaleidoscope of power. The intricacies and intimacies of sandpit life could warrant a volume of musings in their own right, but here I will content myself with divulging a few of the more basic ploys. Your job in the sandpit is to utilise these moves to establish your position as Pit Boss. Good luck.

## 1 The Sprawl
On first entering the sandpit, it is traditional to execute the Sprawl. The aim is to get as much of your body in contact with as much of the sand as possible. The move symbolises an acceptance of The Arena. It is also designed to get the maximum amount of sand into the nooks and crannies of your clothing. (Sand can be retrieved for private use at home).

## 2 The Sand Shower
Alert other players to your arrival by grabbing one or two handfuls of sand and throwing them up in the air so that they fall down into your own hair. It is a move akin to that sumo wrestlers make with talc before they start a bout. It intimidates the opposition as it shows you don't care if you get sand in your eyes.

### 3 The Sand Throw (aimless)

This involves grabbing sand and throwing it about seemingly at random but, as with all things in The Arena of Sand, there is a point. You are marking out territory. You are, if you like, drawing a line in the sand.

### 4 The Sand Throw (targeted)

A powerful move, that often results in tears. It is the one move almost all opponents dread. However, it is also the move that, if spotted by a parent, will result in your instant removal from The Arena. Attempt it rarely, and only when you are out of the parental line of sight.

### 5 Buckets and Spades (discarded)

These must be seized at the earliest opportunity. Once grabbed, wave them in the air, then move them as quickly as possible to a completely different part of the sandpit. The returning member of the bucket-owning class will
a) discover them gone and b) not be able to see them anywhere. Grief usually ensues.

### 6 Buckets and Spades (in use)

Your response depends upon the size of the person using them. If they're smaller than you, appropriate the prize, it's your right. If they're larger than you, try to trick them into handing over the implements by smiling ingratiatingly at them and holding your hand out hopefully. For maximum effect, only attempt this move in front of your opponent's parent, who will often take the bucket or spade from your opponent and give it to you. If your opponent objects to being thus deprived by a parent who should really be on their side, the parent often scolds the opponent, mentioning the dreaded s- word.

## 7 Sand Eating

Another ploy designed to intimidate those around you. Also a good move to try if you think your parents are beginning to look relaxed or are engaging another parent in conversation that has nothing to do with you.

# And You Thought That Guy in Zenda Had A Raw Deal

What am I supposed to have done? What misdemeanour blots my record? What crime am I being punished for? I have scoured my memory yet I can come up with no action on my part, either on purpose or by accident, that warrants the kind of treatment to which I am routinely subjected.

What am I talking about?

Every night I am made to sleep behind bars. Why? I also have no choice as to the time I go to bed. I'm just incarcerated behind the bars and the lights are turned off at a time that is in no way of my choosing. Do I protest? You bet. I scream, I holler, I bang on the bars. Most of the time it's to no avail. Occasionally someone comes in, not to get me out, oh no sirree bob. They come in just to make sure 'I'm alright'.

'Making sure I'm alright' is actually a euphemism for 'making sure they're alright'. I reckon the parents know they're doing wrong by locking me up when there's still loads of playing time to be had, so they come in to assuage their own sense of guilt. I'm the one behind bars, they're the ones who feel guilty.

Going to sleep every night behind bars means that I wake up every morning behind bars. Imagine the long-term psychological damage that does to an individual. I wake, I see the bars and naturally I think that I am bad, that I have done wrong. But as the sleep clears from my mind I realise that it's not me that's bad, it's the system. And I am a victim of the system. Of course I start shouting. It's not a shout for attention, it's a shout for justice.

Next I am carried downstairs, whether I want to go or not, strapped into a chair, and fed. Yes, you heard me right, I am strapped into a chair and fed. I have no choice as to what I'm fed, I get what I'm given. What I'm given is all too often slushy gloop that tastes of wallpaper paste. I'm ashamed to say that so intimidated am I by this point that I usually eat the stuff. Occasionally I will try to register my disapproval at my treatment by knocking the incoming spoon out of the feeder's hand, or by pushing the bowl of gloop over onto the floor. The parents don't like it and it often means the feeding stops so I go hungry. But at least I have established that I am an individual with a free will.

Then I'm taken upstairs again, water is thrown in my face, they try to smother me with a towel and I am dressed. I have no choice in the matter. I am dressed in what has been chosen for me. Then the rest of the day begins. And I have no say over what I get to do. It, too, is decided for me. Where I go, what I do, even who I can associate with, is all dependent on the whims and fancies of Hairy and Smooth.

But I haven't got to the worst bit. Mind control. They try and inculcate in me their own values, beliefs and opinions. It is brainwashing. They try to monitor, censor and control all the intellectual stimuli I encounter. And on the whole they succeed. Which is why it is vital, vital, vital to seek out the stimuli and experiences of which they disapprove. And to be sneaky about it.

No matter how much they admonish (and they will), seize every opportunity to do things they don't want you to, meet people they don't want you to and eat things they don't want you to. Your very individuality depends upon it.

Oh yes, one last thing. They ignore everything I say. Can you imagine how isolating that is? There's no better way to break down a personality than isolation. Imagine how harmful such treatment could be when your personality is actually forming in the first place.

Now that I've documented the strictures of my own private gulag, I can but hope that someone brings the evidence to the attention of Amnesty International. You see, I've finally figured out the crime I committed that condemns me to this life of unjust confinement.

I was born.

That's all, I was born. I had no choice in the matter. In fact, when you think about it, the people who had the choice in the matter were Hairy and Smooth. That's right, my parents, the very people who imprison me now.

Makes you think, doesn't it?

# Rolling Around For No Apparent Reason

This is a game I've invented. What you do is, you lie down on the floor, then propel yourself from side to side of the room simply by rocking your body back and forth. You can use your arms and legs if you must, but it is a technique I frown upon. Not that I'm anally retentive about it. I mean, the game's all about having fun, so if it feels good, do it. There are no rules. There is no real aim. There can be no winners and losers. It's brilliant. You really should try it.

The position you have to get in to start off isn't the most elegant, and if you play the game at all vigorously it can become a touch immodest, but it is wonderful fun. If you're feeling a little shy, maybe try it on your own behind closed doors. Once you get the hang of the basic game you can move on to the more advanced set up, i.e. rolling around on the floor for no apparent reason with somebody else.

Now, look me in the eye and tell me that doesn't sound appealing.

# Just A Cold

**M**y eyes hurt. My nose streams. My body aches. Why? How long will it last? What if this is the way it's going to be from now on?

One minute I'm freezing cold, the next I'm bathed in sweat. My body, my very body, is letting me down.

I scream, I shout, I cry. But nothing happens. I look to the parents for help. But all I see are pained expressions. Concerned stares. Helpless looks. I thrash around in frustration. I fling the proffered toys from my sweaty hands. I tear at my clothes. But there is no respite.

Instead it gets worse. Snot gathers in my head. It hangs around like a gang of malevolent youths on a late-night street corner waiting for a pensioner. As I try to breathe, the snot gets in the way, trips the air up, tries to smother it in a clingy, phlegmy, blanket. But I know I have to keep breathing, have to keep pushing air in and out of my lungs, have to fight the damp hordes of snot.

But it's hard. So hard. And there is no end in sight. A whole day passes like this. Then it's bath time. As the hot water soothes my aching body, and the steam clears my head, I start to think that it's over. But I am wrong. For the bath is just a temporary lull. The snot is merely gathering its forces and regrouping for a new offensive that will rage on and on through the long hours of darkness.

I am taken out of the bath and wrapped in a large warm towel. My body is dried. Minty goo is rubbed into my chest.

I am dressed in more layers of clothes than usual. My bottle contains juice instead of milk. I would point out the mistake but I am too tired to do so. All the while the snot doesn't raise its ugly head. It stays dug in. Maybe it's too tired, and needs a good night's sleep.

I'm carried to my cot and am laid gently down so the soothing balm of sleep can work its magic. And that's when the snot strikes again. Wave after wave leap from the trenches and flood towards me. I struggle up and cry out in horror. I push air furiously through my nose with all the strength I possess. But the snot just keeps on coming, trying to suffocate me in its wet embrace.

Smooth comes into my room. But she can do nothing. This is my battle. I have to win it alone. All night long the conflict rages, terror and dread my constant companions. Eventually, in the early hours, I collapse exhausted into a fitful sleep. I can do no more. What will be, will be. And in the morning, to my amazement, the snot has fled. All that remains is a crusty smear between my nose and my lip.

It is unbelievable. Unbelievable.

I greet Smooth with a joyous shout of victory. But she can hardly raise a smile. She looks dreadful. Now what's all that about? I'm the one who's been through the wars. All Smooth did was watch. I mean it's not as if he did anything to help. Honestly, parents are such wimps at times.

Now, what shall we play today? I know, where's my drum?

# MONTH XV

In which I decide to make a stand and say I am no longer content to subject myself to the indignity of having to meet any pre-set developmental criteria as to my physical, mental and social achievements. I am an individual and I will develop how and when I see fit. If that doesn't match what I should or shouldn't be doing at any specific point in my life, well eat my nappy!

# The Stalker. A Mystery Solved

L ook, if someone had explained to me about mirrors in the first place...

# An Open And Shut Case

**D**oors. I love doors. The way they swing back and forth. The way they open and close. The sound they make. The feel of them. The taste of them. And like everything that we get really excited about, doors are dangerous.

Take today for instance. Hairy and Smooth were, for nefarious purposes of their own, elsewhere. Not that their absences ever last long. No such luck. But this afternoon their guard-duty schedules did not have the same snug-fitting overlap like a too-small sleepy suit that they usually do. Hence, I was presented with a window of opportunity. And one without a safety catch. They're the windows you have to seize with both hands and clamber through as fast as possible.

I surveyed my options. There was stuff I could pull off a shelf. There was a cup that looked like it still might have some coffee in it. There was a big bottle of bleach with the top off - only kidding, just wanted to see if you were paying attention. Then I spied the one that really got my pulses racing: the cupboard door.

A surge of adrenaline spiced with a frisson of danger (my favourite type of frisson) coursed through my body as I clambered full speed towards it. You see, the thing is that doors bite. You innocently put your hand in and they close on you like a rottweiler seizing a kebab.

But the truly glorious thing about this totally unprovoked attack is that it doesn't always happen. There is no discernible pattern. No strict modus operandi. Sometimes the bastard thing bites. Sometimes it doesn't. God, the uncertainty of it all is such a thrill. And it's excitement squared if Hairy and Smooth aren't around because, should the door bite, there's no one nearby to rescue you.

Anyway, the cupboard door it was.

As I approached it, I slowed my pace. No point in appearing over eager. No point in alerting the door until the last possible moment. Near the door handle I paused, affecting a certain insouciance. The door did not react. It gave no clue as to its frame of mind. Cautiously I reached for the handle. It felt cool and comforting. I savoured the moment. Who can describe the instant before an adventure begins? Is it excitement, or hope, or fear?

I took a deep breath. I pulled the handle. The door opened. I pushed the handle. The door closed. I did it again. And again. Bliss.

The door was obviously in a mellow place. No hint of aggression greeted my joyous manipulation. Open. Shut. Open. Shut. Open. Shut. As I lost myself in the revelry of my actions, my mind began to focus on what I was doing. On what it felt like. And why it was such a thrill. What follows is a brief discourse on my musings about why a door is so much more than a physical thing.

# The Doors Of Perception

**W**hat I realised is this. A door is a gateway between two realities. The inside and the outside. The fascinating thing about the world inside the door is that it doesn't exist until I open the door. By opening the door, I have altered the shape of my environment. And — here's the truly fab bit — I can alter it back.

So often when you change the world, you can't change it back. For example, porridge in a bowl knocked onto the floor never gets back in the bowl. It lies in a heap, a monument to the unforgivingly linear one-way nature of time. Likewise, poo that leaks from the side of a nappy can't go back. And so often in life, neither can we. We can only go forward. We seem trapped in a relentless hurtle of events. Life is very simply what happens next.

With a door, you can open it, then you can close it. Once it's closed everything is exactly the same as before you opened it. That's why I see a door as a metaphor for control in a world in which all too often, we have no control.

So pleased was I with the elegance and intricacies of this revelation that I didn't concentrate on what I was doing. The door, noticing my negligence, bit me. Cunning swine. Boy did I scream. But even as I waited in agony for Hairy or Smooth to come to my aid, I couldn't help but reflect that such is life. The most profound philosophical insights must always vie for attention with the physical imperatives of our world. Smooth turned up, opened the cupboard door (why didn't I think of that?) removed my hand, then did what she always does in these situations, i.e. go to eat my fingers, then at the last minute change her mind and just brush them with her lips instead.

How is that supposed to help?

# You Can Keep Your Zippo Lighters, Coke Bottles And Philip Starck Orange Squeezers, Because What I've Just Discovered Is A Real Design Classic

My finger fits up my nose.

# Nursery Crimes Three.
# The Incey Wincey Spider Incident

'Incey Wincey Spider climbed up the water spout,
Down came the rain and washed the spider out.
Out came the sunshine and dried up all the rain.
Incey Wincey Spider climbed up the spout again.'

It is, in its own way, a heartening parable of
perseverance. The plot points are clear and easy to
understand. A spider — probably quite small — climbs up
a water spout. A deluge ensues and the spider is washed
out. But the fortuitous arrival of the sun reverses the
prevailing atmospheric conditions, dries up all the rain, and
allows said spider to resume its journey.

It's a story I can listen to again and again, each time
noticing something fresh in the tale, some subtle nuance,
that gives me pause for thought. And when the whole tale is
told in conjunction with the hand-dance Smooth performs
so admirably, then I am in the thrall of one of the finest
multi-media extravaganzas I have ever encountered.

So what's the problem?

Well, it's this. Mr I. W. Spider is undoubtedly the hero of
the piece. There is much in his enigmatic persona that calls
to mind Clint Eastwood. There are also echoes of Robert The
Bruce's encounter with a most determined arachnid.
Whichever way you visualise or characterise him, Incey is

most definitely the story's main protagonist. And a protagonist one inevitably comes to admire.

Contrast this scenario with one that unfurled earlier today.

Smooth had just extracted a set of car keys from my mouth and was carrying me into the garden to distract me from the wail I was wailing. We exited via the kitchen door. As we passed between tree and wall, we broke a gossamer trip wire laid cunningly across our path. Something small scurried into Smooth's hair. Smooth screamed, all but dropped me, and started frantically clawing at her hair with both hands.

Clearly some great evil had befallen her and she was in terrible danger. She rushed indoors to Hairy, who checked her hair. She calmed down, came back out, and picked me up. And whispered in my ear:

'I hate spiders.'

Is it any wonder I get confused?

# In Which I Get To Grips With Reality And The Symbols With Which That Reality Is Represented And Come To Realise There Is Often A Shortfall Between The Two

I t all started with quack-quacks. At the park. The quack-quacks at the park eat bread. Or don't eat bread, if they don't feel like it. I'd just about come to terms with them, when suddenly something else was competing for the name quack-quack.

These were bright yellow, never ate bread, and lived in the bathroom.

On the face of it the two competing quack-quacks were very different from each other. But both had the same name. As if this was not difficult enough, the matter was further complicated by the appearance of a third entity that was also, apparently, a quack-quack. This third quack-quack was again inanimate, but lived in a book, and was two-dimensional. Yet all three versions aspired to the same title of quack-quack.

I was sitting in the bath pondering this puzzling state of affairs — indeed I was seeing if the bath quack-quacks could fly like the park quack-quacks — when the truth dawned.

The park quack-quacks were the real ones; the other two versions were merely symbolic representations of the original. It was a real road to Damascus moment. The concept that reality could be represented by symbols opened up all sorts of possibilities even to my young mind. If there was one moment that set me on the path to being a writer, this was it. But though euphoria held me in its thrall, a note of caution crept in as the more critical, analytical side of my nature planted an intriguing question.

'How come quack-quacks in books and in bathrooms are invariably yellow, and quack-quacks down the park never are?'

# Teletubbies. The Inside Track

I have discussed the matter with many of my colleagues and the consensus is that the Teletubbies are the genuine article. Tinky-Winky, Dipsy, La-La and Po are my generation's equivalent of John, Paul, George and Ringo. You may protest that lyrically and in terms of sheer musicality the Fat Four can't compete with the Fab Four, but I beg to differ. I mean, is 'Teletubbies say eh-oh. Eh-oh' any more inane than 'She loves you, yeah, yeah, yeah'?

Okay, so the Beatles did go on to construct the glorious abstraction of 'A Day In The Life', but that was much later on in their careers. All I'm saying is you need to give the Teletubbies a bit of time to develop. And in one way the Fat Four are already way ahead. Namely, the Beatles had to indulge in mind-altering and consciousness-expanding substances before they started fishing in the electric duckpond of psychedelic imagery. The Teletubbies, however, operate in a world that right from day one out-surreals anything in 'Lucy In The Sky With Diamonds'.

However, it must be said that the devotion and sheer excitement with which my generation collects and hoards Tubbierebilia extends far beyond the realms of mere fandom. So what, precisely, is going on? Why are the Teletubbies the phenomenon they are?

Well, the answer is so simple that no one has spotted it. The real power of the Teletubbies is nothing to do with

Tinky-Winky, Dipsy, La-La or Po. They are merely the front that has been created behind which the Universal Truth can be spread. And the Universal Truth, like all the most profound philosophies, is propagated via metaphor. If you're still at a loss as to what I'm going on about, consider how the programme starts. And how it ends. It starts when the sun rises. And it ends when the sun sets. And the sun is a baby.

Think about it.

# In At The Shallow End

Today I went on my first trip to a swimming pool. Surreal or what? Essentially a swimming pool is like a giant bath. Except that while you are put into the bath with no clothes on, you're put into the swimming pool with a rather snazzy, lightweight, streamlined nappy.

On entering the pool you are immediately struck by the fact that it is neither as hot as a bath, nor are there any bubbles. Closer inspection reveals that there are none of the yellow quack-quacks (in varying size) that are synonymous with the bathtub/bathtime experience.

Also, and this is a tad more perturbing, the pool has no bottom. There's nothing to sit or stand on. You are totally dependent on the parent you go with to keep your head out of the water. Strangely, I found this lack of bottom liberating, not terrifying. Partly this is due to the fact that I had a growing conviction that the parent (which on my first visit was Smooth) would not let me go under. It was a reassuring conviction totally at odds with how Smooth treats me the rest of the time.

But the really bizarre twist to the whole scenario was the presence of other people and parents in the water. I kid you not. There were other people in there. People I had never met before in my entire life. Crazy or what?

At first their presence rendered me a little shy but as time went by I warmed to the situation. It was kind of fun. And emboldened by this 'anything goes' spirit, I thought I'd try a little experiment. I splashed.

Now splashing, as everyone knows, is way out of order. It's pretty high up on the list of behaviours guaranteed to get Hairy and Smooth in a strop. To splash in the bath is a major misdemeanour. So when I splashed in the swimming pool I was, to say the least, pushing my luck.

I raised one arm in the air, then the other, then brought them both down simultaneously in an overhead, open-palmed, two-handed smash that, if ever attempted in the bath, would have resulted in an immediate early towel. As my hands hit the water I knew I was skating on very thin ice.

They touched down with a thwack as glorious as it was loud. Water rose majestically upwards, glittered in the sunlight like a shower of diamonds, then fell back exhausted to join the rest of its brethren. It was glorious. In slow motion I felt my head turn toward Smooth as I waited for my no doubt deserved rebuke. But the rebuke never came. Instead Smooth was laughing. And smiling. And, get this, started to splash too.

Is it any wonder I started crying?

What else are you supposed to do when your world is suddenly turned upside down. We went home. I was very subdued in the bath that night. It was all just too crazy. I slept restlessly, concerned about what the day ahead would hold.

# When You Can Grab The Stone From My Hand Before I Close It, Then You Can Leave The Monastery, Glasshopper

Picture the scene. You have a cold. Snot runs from your nose like the Mongol hordes of yore streaming across the Russian Steppes hell bent on bringing doom, gloom and despond to all in their path. Hairy holds a tissue.

You, as is your nature, will attempt to run the snot from nose to chin to chest in one continuous oleaginous stream. Hairy will attempt to frustrate this impressive feat of fluid engineering with a selfish quasi-fascistic tissue intervention.

Do not, I repeat, do not, allow this to happen.

Turn your head, twist your body, punch, claw, wriggle, kick. Do whatever you have to do. Just keep that tissue away. It's you or Hairy. And there can only be one winner. But if you see no escape from the approaching tissue, do not despair.

You have one last shot in the chamber.

You won't win. But you won't lose. You may be smaller than Hairy, but like Drake's ships taking on the large galleons of the Spanish Armada, you're faster and more manoeuverable. So, as the tissue looms it's up with your arm, place the sleeve of whatever you're wearing adjacent to your nasal area, then rapidly pull arm, sleeve and back of hand across the nose.

Wear your snot with pride. You've earned it. And should you want to rub it in, rub it in. All over the Hairy's clothes. He'll hate that.

# For Six Months I Thought My Name Was 'Gently'

It was all I heard. Wherever I went, whatever I did, before long that is what would be shouted at me. There I'd be, merrily investigating the bangy properties of a telephone receiver against a wall, when said receiver would be snatched from my enquiring hand and the 'G' word barked at me. Or I'd be in the sandpit quietly explaining to a colleague why they should really relinquish control of a spade, when Smooth would dive towards me with the word brandished in front of her like an electric cattle prod.

It was shouted at me so often that I started to worry when it wasn't. When that happened I'd have to do something that warranted the admonition just to reassure myself that everything was right with the world. Then, like all things you hear over and over, it started to lose all meaning. It was just a sound. And it made me contemplate the connection between sounds and words, between words and sounds.

The conclusion I came to is that words are sound symbols designed to be used for communication purposes.

This inevitably led to some frustration on my part because at that point in my development, while I could undoubtedly make sounds, I couldn't make words. I was stuck in a world of a fairly limited range of noises and quite a small choice of intonations.

If I could only master words then I could begin to get a

purchase on what was really going on.

However, one nagging doubt hangs about in my mind. I'm kind of afraid that when I do master words and can communicate more fully with my parents I'm going to find out that they are, how can I put this politely, just a little bit slow. Maybe I'm being over sensitive, but the basis of my concern lies in the books they share with me. It's obvious these are their favourite books, because they return to them time after time. But as works of literature they hardly tax the brain. I mean the one about the five little ducks going swimming one day — well the characterisation is very weak, the plot is feeble and the supposed twist at the end isn't exactly Hitchcockian.

However, if it keeps the parents happy, who am I to question its validity? Maybe it's a matter I'll have to raise with them in years to come. And when I do I suppose I'll have to do it...gently.

# One Small Step

I t's 1969. The end of the decade in which President Kennedy chose to go to the moon. And the Eagle has landed. Blurry pictures are beamed back across the lifeless void. Millions sit glued to their TVs to witness the historic first steps of man on an alien planet. A slow-motion Neil Armstrong descends the ladder to plant his feet finally on The Sea of Tranquillity. As he takes his 'one small step' he utters the words that will live on in history.

Well, bully for you Neil. You were lucky. You had someone listening.

Can you imagine how frustrating it is to achieve something that is, in a very real sense, just as historic and, I would argue, more world-changing, and not be able to communicate your thoughts to those around you? That is precisely the predicament the novice walker is faced with. They are trapped by the cruel juxtaposition of their sudden ability to walk with their inability to talk.

Which is why, when faced with the stunned, excited and adoring faces that invariably greet our first steps, we inevitably can do little more than beam delightedly. Hardly a fitting vehicle to convey the maelstrom of conflicting thoughts and emotions that swirl within us as we take our first steps in the world. Which is why I welcome this opportunity to set the record straight and lay before you some of the thoughts that ran through my head as I first walked:

1. Yeeeeessssssssssssss!

2. Wooooooahhhhhhhhh!

3. No seat belt? No brakes? This can't be right?

4. Gosh, it's a long way down.

5. Hey, it's not so difficult.

6. Now they're in trouble.

7. Marsupial, that's an odd word.

8. Why is everything and everyone wobbling?

9. Must be an earthquake.

10. My hands are free!

11. Watch out for that knee.

12. I could get to like this.

13. Now where did I drop that rusk?

14. Wait till they see me down the sandpit.

15. Hey, let's open her up and see how fast this thing goes.

16. Coming through, coming through!

17. Who put that there?

In all I took three steps.

And while the thoughts that slammed through my head were inevitably the product of the euphoria of the experience, I had taken the precaution of preparing a little speech that I would like to have made if only there had been any way of getting myself understood. What follows is the text of that speech:

*The first steps in any endeavour are always the most important. For without the first steps no journey can ever be made. I take my first steps in joy, in trepidation and in hope. And I will try to make my journey an exploration of the possible, an exhortation of delight and an example for those yet to come. Success or failure in my endeavours are outcomes that lie far over the misty horizon that is the road ahead. For now I am just grateful that in the journey that is my life, I have taken my first steps.*

But I had to make do with a stupid smile.

# MONTH XVI

And to think I used to believe that crawling was the state-of-the-art in the personal mobility stakes.

# Walking Changes Everything

I used to crawl, but now I walk. More precisely, I totter, I stagger, I often stumble. I am new at this game and my skill is minimal. I understand the principles, I have a grasp of the aesthetics, but it's the practical application that is so frustratingly elusive.

Walking is fantastic. Even though I'm crap at it. Walking changes everything. I have moved from a world of shins to a world of knees. This is hardly a quantum leap, but it's a step (ho-ho) in the right direction. Crawling around looking at shins all day does not give you a particularly favourable impression of humanity. Knees, on the other hand, are completely different.

Knees conjure up a world in which the existence of a jointed limb has led to so much. A world of running and jumping and kicking. A world of stamping flamenco, sensual ballet and all the works of the incomparable Mr Fosse. A world of kneeling, with all that encompasses in terms of religious and regal supplication. And a world which can give us the glory of The Ministry Of Funny Walks.

So now that I have access to this world of knees is it any wonder that I rejoice in my elevation from quadruped to biped?

# I Love The Smell Of Nappies In The Morning, They Smell Of...Victory

I rise in the dark. All around me is silence. Sleep cradles me in its gentle grip. I close my eyes and drift off again. I slip into the soft surreality of dreams created by a mind that is still, even in its waking moments, only just forming. The world when I am awake is often a bizarre, jumbled, disconnected, nonsensical place. So the dreams I dream are strange indeed. But I know that they are my dreams. (I'm with Ringo on that one.) They're definitely my dreams.

I open my eyes again. All is as it was. Except now a little light seeps in from around the curtains over the window. I stare towards it for a while, then decide to explore my cot. I know full well what is in here, but it is a ritual in which I occasionally indulge as a way of reassuring myself. I stretch out a foot and encounter the bars. They are hard and unyielding. But there are gaps between them. I have long thought that in this arrangement of bars and gaps that there is a metaphor for life. Whatever we try to achieve in life, there are always bars barring our way. But there are also always gaps. In pessimistic mode, I wallow in the knowledge that the gaps are invariably too small to crawl through. When optimism prevails, I tell myself that there's always a big enough gap, somewhere. I just have to find it.

I stick my feet through the bars and bang them back and forth a bit. It hurts, but it's real. Pain is real. And this pain is under my control. It so often isn't.

I reach out my hand and find Teddy Bear. I pull him towards me. He looks like he's had a pretty rough night. In my heart of hearts I know that Teddy Bear is just a toy. But in my heart of heart of hearts I know that he is much more than that. Frankly, you can't have been through all the stuff we've been through together without forming some very real kind of bond. Not that Teddy Bear ever expresses any feelings in this (or any other) area. He's much too enigmatic an individual to do anything so blatant. (I'm also beginning to suspect that he can't actually talk.) I lift Teddy Bear towards my mouth and suck on his ear to reassure him of the deep, quasi-mystical nature of our friendship. He says nothing.

The gloom that tends to hang listlessly about the room every morning finally starts to collect its things and make its excuses. The room, my room, has once again tidied itself up. This transformation, though incredible, has become so common place, that these days I hardly notice it at all. But when I do, it still amazes me. Indeed sometimes I am so intrigued by the self-tidying room phenomenon, that I try and make as much mess as possible during the day, and especially just before I go to bed, in order to see if the S.T.R.. can handle it. And it always can. It is truly remarkable.

A low-level feeling of discomfort begins to creep over me. It takes me a while to figure out the exact nature of the problem, so, not wanting to waste time in getting the issue resolved, I am already mid-wail before I realise that I have once again fallen prey to that perennial bugbear, my old nemesis, that Lex Luthor to my Superman — poo.

The door to my room opens and Hairy appears in a blinding light. The sudden intensity of illumination hurts my eyes and I

wail even louder. Hairy makes conciliatory
noises. His demeanour reveals the fact that he
has just stumbled from his own bed, and
indeed, his own dreams. He reaches towards
me and rubs my back. He means well, but nice
though the occasional back rub is, it doesn't
really address the issue at hand. (Or at
nappy.) I wail louder still.

Hairy picks up Teddy Bear, pushes him towards me, and
informs me that Teddy Bear is here. I give Hairy a look that I
hope conveys the following sentiment:'Yes, you oaf, I do indeed
know that Teddy Bear is here but much as I love Teddy Bear
(which I do), he can't really help me out in my current
predicament on account of him having no fingers and on the
whole being largely inanimate.' Whether Hairy got all that from
my look I can't really say.

I wailed louder still.

The door opened again and Smooth appeared. Smooth and
Hairy had a brief discussion that ended with Smooth giving
Hairy a look that seemed to communicate quite a lot in a very
brief period. Hairy left the room in a sulk. Smooth soon got to
the bottom of the matter. And got the matter off the bottom.
And as I lay on the cool changing mat, my legs in the air and
my nether regions exposed to the soothing balm of an icy wet
wipe, a thought occurred to me.

I had made this happen. I, through the medium of a full and
rather smelly nappy, had made this happen. I had summoned
first Hairy, and then Smooth, from their bed and made them
tend to my needs. All because I had woken with poo in my
pants. Now that's power.

# Walking Changes Everything. (Again)

It's the hands-free thing.

Now that I can walk I can get around and have my hands free to either do things, or carry things. This is an incredible boon as I find myself smack-bang in the middle of a period when, for some unfathomable reason, it is imperative that I carry the remote control for the television wherever I go. Don't ask me why. And yes I do know it doesn't work in the other rooms.

While I was stuck in the slow lane of the motorway of life, where crawling is your only option, the necessary engagement of all four limbs when in crawl mode made carrying the remote control challenging. For a short while, before I figured out precisely what was going on, I'd find that clinging onto the remote while trying to actively crawl led me to do little more than go round in circles. Quite embarrassing really.

But now all such unsatisfactory shenanigans are behind me. I can walk and carry at the same time.

I have now managed to show the remote control all kinds of rooms and places it has never ever seen before. The other day, for instance, I even managed to get it a go on the swings in the park. Bizarrely, however, neither Hairy or Smooth seem to appreciate my achievement in expanding the remote control's horizons and are forever prising it from my grasp.

# On Crying. Two Methods Guaranteed To Elicit The Biggest Response

Crying, in my opinion, should be a tactic of last resort. Cry too early or cry too often, and you lose the initiative and lessen the immediacy of your demands. My advice is to try all other available avenues first; if they fail, then cry. Having said that I must admit I do occasionally cry at the start of a transaction just to shake things up a bit. (I've noticed that if Hairy or Smooth discern a pattern in my behaviour, they inevitably try to exploit it to my disadvantage.)

What I'm saying is, don't cry too often. Or there'll be no one listening. Or worse still, there'll be people listening, but they won't do anything. Which is why I'd like to share with you two advanced crying techniques.

## The Silent Wail with Brimming Eyes

This is in two parts. The first involves opening your mouth as wide as you can, straining every muscle in your face to emit the loudest sound imaginable and then, and here's the revolutionary bit, not making a sound! The strength of this manoeuvre lies in the fact that it is a total reversal of the norm. Deconstruct the action and the subtext is , 'I'm so unhappy that I can't even cry'. Sheer genius. I take my bib off to whoever came up with that one. But it gets better. Having hooked the suckers with The Silent Wail, you reel them in with the second part, The Brimming Eyes. This technique involves starting to cry, but not allowing the tears to fall. Instead, catch them in the bottom of your eyelids and let them gather there. (It's a tricky skill but well worth hours of private practice to perfect.) Put the two together, and you get the Silent Wail with Brimming Eyes. You can't lose: it's like having Pelè and Cruyff on the same team.

## The U-Shaped Tongue

If due to unforeseen circumstances The Silent Wail with Brimming Eyes fails to jerk a heartstring, try this failsafe technique. Open your mouth to let loose a standard cry of anguish, but as you do raise both the sides and the tip of your tongue; tricky but not impossible. The second part of the move is even more fiendish: keeping the sides and the tip of the tongue raised, get the whole thing to quiver tentatively. A devilish hard act to master but the dismay it causes the opposition has to be seen to be believed.

NB If neither of these techniques brings results, it's probably best for you to shut up. It may mean a new series of ER has just started in the other room in which case your chances of getting Smooth to do anything at all for at least the next hour are zilch.

# How Walking Enables You To Improve Your Game In The Leg-Clinging Department

Leg-clinging is a skill that is simplicity itself. You approach your target individual, grab the leg, tilt your head upwards, then like a baby bird in the nest demanding to be fed, you open your mouth and wail.

It's a cracking manoeuvre that almost always gets results. Unless your target extricates their leg and moves away. Then you have to crawl towards them once again and repeat the whole process. Unfortunately crawling involves both arms, as does clinging. This gives Hairy or Smooth the advantage of being able to nip about while you're still trying to figure out whether to focus on crawling or grabbing. It is reminiscent of the mighty Muhammad Ali dancing round one of his more cumbersome opponents.

However, help is at hand. Or, more correctly, at foot. Or, more correctly still, at feet.

Once you can walk, those cunning swine can't get away from you. By delegating locomotive duties solely to the legs and feet, and grabbing and clinging functions to the arms and hands, you will find yourself more than a match for your opponent. When they try to move away, you just go with them, wail uninterrupted. What's even better, because you're actively clinging onto the leg, you don't actually have to be any good at walking to benefit from this scenario.

# Nursery Crimes Four. How On Earth Has Old McDonald Survived So Long?

'Old McDonald had a farm,
Ee-aye, ee-aye, oh
And on that farm he had a
Sheep/pig/cow/duck/hen/cat/dog/ [delete as applicable]
Ee-aye, ee-aye, oh'

So let me get this straight. Old McDonald had a farm. And on this farm he had, by all accounts, a sheep, a pig, a cow, a duck, a hen, a cat, a dog, and according to some texts, a mouse. That means, pets and pests aside, when it came to livestock he basically had one of each animal. Now call me an unfeeling capitalist in the pocket of multinational megacorporate agri-business if you like, but that doesn't sound a terribly efficient way to farm. I mean how long can it be before,

'And on that farm he had a foreclosure notice,
Eee-aye, eee-aye, oh-no',

is heard down at Old McDonald's place?

My point being that, as an instructive tale for impressionable minds, it's not the most economically sound lesson I've ever come across. Generations have grown up learning the rhyme by rote from a very early age: is it any wonder that the farming industry tends towards periodic crises?

# Walking Changes Things
## (Not Always In A Good Way)

You fall over more often. You fall further.

# When To Run.
## (Don't Believe The Hype)

You may come across the maxim 'Don't try to run before you can walk'.

I disagree. I reckon it's worth a try. While it may be very unlikely that you would succeed, what if you did? Imagine the admiring looks you would gather as you flitted hither and thither around the sandpit in the park. Imagine, on a more mercenary note, the sponsorship deals you could command. A baby that could actually run before it could walk? If that didn't get the top bananas of Nike flying in on their Lear jets with cheque books awaving, I would be one exceedingly surprised individual.

Sadly, when I did try to run before I could walk, it all went decidedly pear-shaped on me. But the important thing is that I tried. As my people say, 'If you never suck the teat, you'll never get the milk.'

I digress. What I really want to share with you is the advice that once you've got those first few, tentative steps out of the way, run as soon as possible. Running is brilliant. Running is like walking, only faster. Running gives you all the benefits of walking, except it takes less time. Which, when you come to think about it, means that in any given amount of time you can get further. Running shrinks the world. Marvellous.

The best thing about running however cannot be defined in such logical terms. That's because the best thing is the sheer physical thrill of it. It is a joy, an unadulterated joy. Until you fall over, of course. But let's face it, nothing this much fun can go on forever.

# The Clean Bib/Dirty Bib Routine

A strange phenomenon occurs at meal times. It concerns that most hated of neckwear, the old biberooni. Why on earth do they insist on putting one on me when it is obvious that I am already perfectly well attired? I try my best to twist away from the imposition of yet another item of clothing but after a while I let them have their way. I mean, to me, in the end, it's no big thing. And if it's so important to them that I wear it, well, why not? Life's too short.

I suppose it's a dress code thing: you can't eat here unless you've got the right clothes. To my way of thinking this is a most bourgeois and outdated approach to what should be a simple pleasure i.e. eating. Far be it from me to point out that these days even many of the finest Michelin starred hostelries refrain from imposing on their patrons anything as establishmentarian as a dress code.

But I've noticed a particularly peculiar aspect of the whole bib matter: there seems to be two types of bib – the dirty bib, and the much rarer clean bib. The other night, as I mooched around the old cot before succumbing to a directive from the People's Republic of Nod, I tried to fathom out if there was any reason why which bib appeared when. What I did – and I'm rather proud of this pioneering research – was to try and correlate the appearance of the rarer, clean bib with

external factors.

What I discovered is that the clean bib, the spotless bib, the pristine bib, only ever puts in an appearance when visitors come to the house.

I ask you, what's all that about?

# The Secret Bath

In many ways it is my very own Stonehenge. Why is it there? What is it for? Who built it?

At first, it appeared to be nothing more than another piece of furniture. In form, it is chair-like. However, unlike the other chairs I have encountered, its texture is hard and cold. Also unlike other chairs, it can't be moved.

This is not the first time that I've come across a thing that resembles another thing, but is, in fact, a completely different thing. Indeed it could be argued that a very large part of the growing and development process in which I am currently enmeshed is about learning to differentiate between things that are, on many levels, largely the same. For instance, Hairy and Smooth are very much alike. Each has two arms, two legs, one head etc. But that is analysis on the macro level. Examine each on a micro level, and it's not the similarities, but the differences that resonate.

For example, when Hairy visits the bathroom he invariably takes with him that large foldy paper thing he stares at in the morning while I'm having my porridge, and he's gone for ages. In contrast, Smooth doesn't take anything with her and returns much more quickly. Why? Who knows.

Or take their very names. Hairy is called 'Hairy' because he is hairy. Smooth is called 'Smooth' because she is smooth. Hairy's face is hairy, his legs are hairy, even his nose is hairy. Smooth's face isn't hairy, neither are her legs, nor her nose. Bizarrely, however, her head is much hairier than Hairy's.

I suppose I am beginning to realise that I live in a world where things can exist in a state of being the same, but different, at one and the same time. Or, to approach the situation from a different path, when is a chair not a chair? When it's got a lid.

Yes, the chair I've been talking about has got a lid. What's more, the lid isn't the end of the story. That's because under the lid, which up until now I had taken to be the seat of the chair, was another lid. But it was a lid unlike any lid I had ever encountered. It was lid with a hole in it. Why two lids when surely one would do? And what use is a second lid at all if it has a massive hole in it?

I was still puzzling over the double-lid mystery when I happened to glance down into the chair. What I saw stunned me. Because what I saw was a limpid pool of crystal clear water. I had discovered a Secret Bath.

# The Secret Bath. I Delve Deeper

I stared in wonder at the marvel I had discovered. Unlike water from the big bath, which is always covered in bubbles, the Secret Bath water was so stunningly clear and beautiful that you'd think Hairy or Smooth would want to show it off. Yet they kept it hidden away.

Maybe they didn't know about the Secret Bath. And if they truly didn't know about it, should I let them in on the secret? I pondered my options. Not letting them know about the Secret Bath would give me a certain amount of power over them; which would be kind of fun. But the Secret Bath was so glorious a thing that keeping it to myself would be such an egotistical act that I would feel diminished.

On the other hand, if they did know about it, and hadn't told me, what kind of light does that cast on them? Not a very good light. That's what kind of light. I have to admit that it wouldn't be entirely out of character for them. You see, I regret to inform you, they can be incredibly selfish.

Anyway, I decided that I would share my discovery with them. After all, I didn't want to end up like that bloke who discovered America before Columbus but decided to keep it to himself. Who remembers him?

I looked from the Secret Bath to the big bath and back again. Time for a little experimentation. I picked up one of the yellow quack-quacks that lives on the side of the big bath. I dropped the quack-quack into the Secret Bath. It fitted perfectly! What joy. Maybe the Secret Bath was a quack-quack retreat, a place to go for some peace and quiet away from the other quack-quacks.

I let the quack-quack enjoy itself for a while and then fished it out. I stared once more into the crystal clear water. It sparkled like a sparkly thing and glimmered like a glimmery thing. And that's when realisation dawned upon me (like a dawny thing). Surely the Secret Bath was my bath! After all, it was just my size.

I leant over the side and extended my arms. My fingers just reached the magical water. It felt fabulous. I raised my heels as high as they would go and pushed off with my toes. For a split second I hung in perfect equilibrium. Then gravity took a hold and I started to topple forwards. I prepared to savour every blissful sensation.

That's when Hairy came into the room. His voice reverberated around the four walls like an explosion. His hands grabbed me and yanked me up into the air. I started to cry. Smooth ran into the room, took me in her arms and held me tight. Through my tears, forgetting that I couldn't really speak, I tried to explain to her about the Secret Bath. But she didn't understand.

As she carried me out of the room, I turned back to cast a look at the scene of all the drama. Hairy was shaking his head and closing the lid of the Secret Bath. Closing both lids. So, I surmised, not only was the Secret Bath secret, it was also forbidden.

Which only makes it all the more intriguing.

# MONTH XVII

Are inside and outside just two sides of the same coin?
And if they are, what, precisely, is on the edge of the coin?

# Two Worlds

You're either inside or you're outside. Inside is primarily defined by floors, walls and ceilings. Outside is primarily defined by a lack of floors, walls and ceilings. Connecting inside and outside are doors. Or sometimes windows. For some unspecified reason, windows are somewhat frowned upon by Hairy and Smooth as a means of movement between these two parallel states of being.

So let's talk about floors. Floors are the defining parameter of inside with which I am most au fait. That is because floors are, in a very real sense, the stage upon which I have acted out most of the drama that comprises my life. The first time I crawled, I was on a floor. The first time I walked, I was on a floor. And the first time I fell over backwards and discovered that my head wasn't exactly what you would call bouncy, I was on a floor. A very hard floor.

Which brings me to one of the intriguing things about floors — they come in a wide variety of finishes. There are hard, vicious, painful floors. There are soft, furry, playful floors. There are wet, slippy, glamorous floors. And there is a strange, ephemeral floor made up of bits of porridge and rusk and gloop that appears mysteriously under my high chair when I eat.

Walls, it has to be said, show less variation. The colours may be different, the textures may vary slightly, but they are generally much of a muchness. Ceilings are duller still. However, I am of the opinion that this very dullness, far from being a fundamental character flaw is in fact a big plus. Dullness gives ceilings a most soothing and calm-inducing quality. Why this should be a good thing? Consider just one question.

When is it that you spend most time looking up at a ceiling?

When you are lying in your cot about to go to sleep. And what's the last thing you want at that precise moment? Stimulation. Which is why the fundamental dullness of ceilings reveals the workings of a design genius at the height of their powers.

The other thing about inside is that it is a more controlled environment than outside. Which is why it is vital that you cross the threshold from inside to outside whenever the opportunity presents itself. Or even when the opportunity doesn't present itself.

Climbing out of the window is my own particular favourite.

# Nursery Crimes Five.
# What Kind Of Role Model Is That?

'Little Miss Muffet
Sat on a tuffet
Eating her curds and whey.
Down came a spider
And sat down beside her
And frightened Miss Muffet away'

What a wuss.

# Teething Problems

I f you're a tadpole, do you know what's about to happen to you? Or does the growth of legs come as a surprise? I mean, there you are, merrily swishing your tail back and forth, cruising among the pond weed, algae and amoebas (amoebi?), when you idly look down and suddenly discover that you have sprouted leglets. What is the thought that splashes across your mind at this precise moment?

**A.** About time.
or
**B.** Oh my God! I'm a freak. Why me? What have I ever done to deserve this? My life is ruined. The other tadpoles are all going to laugh at me. I'm just going to have to spend the rest of my life holed up in the reeds like Gloria Swanson in *Sunset Boulevard.*

I direct your mind to this quandary because it's time we talked about teething. I have been teething off and on for quite a while. But it's kicking in big time right about now. The big boys at the back are coming through.

Cutting that first tooth was, and please excuse my language here, a complete swine. Take it from me, Rod Stewart was right, the first cut is the deepest. Up until then my mouth was, on the whole, a soft and squidgy place. Then this appalling lump of ivory bursts through my gums and takes up residence in my mouth. It was like *Alien* all over again.

Except the damned thing didn't have the courtesy to rush off squealing into the distance, but stayed exactly where it was, exuding a kind of malevolent malice as if to say 'come and have a go if you think you're hard enough'. Quite frankly, it was an appalling intrusion.

I let my feelings be known in the time-honoured fashion.

Apparently, nothing could be done. I was stuck with it.

The eruption of that first tooth, like a mini Matterhorn thrown up by the subterranean clashing of tectonic plates, was bad enough. But worse was to come. When I stopped wailing the wail of a very unhappy waily thing and closed my mouth. Because that's when hard tooth at the bottom of my mouth, met soft gum at the top. Once again I registered my displeasure. It was all going so horribly wrong. My mouth, so long a source of unalloyed pleasure, had turned into a gaping chasm of pain. Surely this couldn't be the way things were supposed to develop?

But it was. And it did. And it didn't stop at just the one tooth. Soon others started turning up like lagered-up louts gatecrashing a coffee morning. And like that very first tooth, these newcomers bristled with surly, swaggering confidence. The tone of the whole neighbourhood started to look decidedly un- 'up and coming'. My mouth, hitherto no slouch in the dribbling stakes, suddenly turned into a veritable Niagara of drool. Whenever I looked down at whatever I was wearing, all I could see was an ever-expanding dark patch starting just below my chin; on one memorable occasion, it made it as far as my knees. And when my mouth wasn't dribbling, my bottom was. (N.B. This strikes me as an appallingly unfair turn of events, I mean the teeth are popping up in my mouth yet it's my bottom that joins in wholeheartedly. Why?) Then there were the seemingly endless bouts of constant, nagging pain. Quite frankly, the whole teething thing was an utter nightmare.

Which is why I got into the whole biting thing. Whenever Hairy or Smooth brought their fingers anywhere near my mouth, I would clamp the old incisors down on them like a crocodile at a watering hole snatching an unsuspecting impala. Don't get me wrong, I wasn't embarking on this behaviour as an act of mindless aggression. Far from it. All I was trying to do was impress upon them that this is what teething feels like.

I'm not sure they got the message.

# Mittens.
# What Bright Spark Invented Them, Then?

**M**ittens are strait-jackets for the fingers. I stare at
the damned things in disbelief. How am I supposed
to pick anything up with them on? How am I
supposed to grab Smooth's hair in that firm but
affectionate way that I have? And, indeed, how am I
supposed to stick any one of my fingers up either of my
nostrils?

Is it any wonder I'm always trying to get the blasted things
off?

I'm sure there must be a whole section on mittens in the
Universal Declaration Of Human Rights. And if there isn't,
there should be.

# Creative Clambering. How To Extend Your Sphere Of Influence Through The Cunning Use Of Chairs

T he world is all the wrong height. There are work surfaces I can't reach. There are shelves I can't get to. There are tables that remain as inaccessible as most restaurants are to someone in a wheelchair. You know that expression about something going straight over someone's head? Well, amongst my people it's not so much a saying as a way of life.

Which brings me to chairs. The whole point of a chair is to give you something to sit upon. It is, I think you'll agree, a wholly admirable purpose. Without chairs there would surely be no sofas. And without sofas and the gaps between their cushions, where would you keep the remote control for the TV? But I digress.

I've discovered another, and I would argue even better, use for the chair. I've discovered that chairs are great for standing on. Stand on a chair and you're instantly taller. Stand on a chair and things denied you because of your lack of stature suddenly become available. Knives you couldn't reach can now be easily grasped. Cups you could only stare at can now be upended and their contents, contents you could only up until now dream about, can be spread out and examined. Switches and plugs you'd never even seen before can now be played with.

Better still, chairs are movable objects. They're not easily movable, but they are movable. Not only is the previously height-restricted world of the immediate environs of the chair accessible, but so are the surroundings of anywhere you can drag, push or slide the chair to.

Of course, in a world as badly designed as ours every silver lining has a cloud. And this innovative use of the chair is no different. Let's just say that never forget that the higher you climb, the further there is to fall.

And in my experience pride doesn't come before a fall, it usually gets squashed underneath it in an undignified heap.

# No

Interesting word. Wonder what it means?

# Dinner And A Show. How To Get More Bang For Your Buck At Meal Times

**W**hy settle for a meal when, with just a little effort, you can get so much more? All that's required of you is a bout of well-timed head turning and some determined mouth clamping.

Like so many situations you encounter when dealing with the likes of Hairy and Smooth, it's a battle of wills. And, gratifyingly, they invariably blink first. Especially Hairy. All I have to do is jut my bottom lip out even a fraction and the big doofus crumbles. It's like taking candy from an adult.

Anyway, so you're in the chair, and you've spurned the proffered gloop. All you have to do is sit tight and the show will come to you. What's more, you're slap bang in the middle of the front row of the stalls. Usually you have a choice of two entertainments.

First, there's what I like to think of as 'supper theatre'. This involves the feeder disappearing momentarily then returning with a book and enacting the story within solely for the amusement and delectation of the feedee. Your part of the deal as the feedee is that while being entertained you do actually eat something. But here's the cunning bit: if you pace your munching and slurping at a pretty pedestrian amble, you can usually get two, three or even more books read to you in the

course of one meal. My own personal record is seventeen. But it took a lot of effort. And after this encounter Hairy (well, who else would it be) had his confidence so shaken that it was a long time indeed before he ventured to confront me in the chair again.

Occasionally, just occasionally, the feeder will resort to The New Book. The New Book is any book that you've never seen before. It's rare, so you can't expect it to happen very often, but when it does enjoy it. Because I believe the appearance of the New Book is symbolic of total capitulation on the part of your adversary. So be gracious in victory. Watch the show, eat the food, and try to keep smugness to yourself.

Second there's 'cabaret'. This involves a lot of singing and fair amount of dance, all of it pretty dire. You'll get nothing by the Beatles, nothing by Sondheim, and nothing from Kurt Weil's golden era. You do occasionally get The Teletubby Song so it's not all bad. Cabaret seems to be pretty much the preserve of Smooth. When Hairy attempts it, he invariably forgets the words of what he's singing or gets them hopelessly muddled. Last week he made a complete Horlicks of 'The Wheels On The Bus'. He got as far as the wheels on the bus going round and round. (Round and round, round and round.) Then it all went hazy on him. That's why next up we had the conductor on the bus collecting everyone's fares. Closely followed up by the inspector on the bus fining everyone who had the wrong ticket. I was aghast at the incompetence of the whole ludicrous performance. And I bolted my food. It was either that or sit there and wait for 'Nelly The Elephant' to die a slow, painful death.

# The Sky Is Crying

It happens a lot and I don't understand why. The tears that fall are cold tears. Sometimes they are fine and soft. Sometimes they are fat and hard and angry. Why the sky is crying is a mystery. What could it have run into? Who could it be missing?

Sometimes when the sky is crying I tilt my face upwards and catch the tears on my cheeks, so that the sky's tears become my tears and I try to feel what the sky is feeling. But it never works. So I never know why the sky is crying.

# MONTH XVIII

Just when I was beginning to worry about there being no
arc to my story (and if there was no arc how was I going to
sell the movie rights to Hollywood), we went on holiday.
Of course, I didn't know we'd gone on holiday.
I thought we'd moved.

# Going On Holiday. Having Fewer Things In A Strange Place

Now I am not an overly materialistic individual. That's why it came as a quite considerable shock that I wailed like a banshee while we were on holiday, when I realised that going on holiday is all about having fewer things.

It started off as just another trip in the car. Admittedly it was a long trip, so long that on several occasions I found myself shouting out 'are we there yet?' Unfortunately, as I am still unable to talk, I don't think Hairy or Smooth really understood what I was asking. I suppose my question came over as little more than an irritating bawl. But such is life.

Eventually, just as we were pulling up outside a strange house, I nodded off. I never realised travel could be so exhausting. It's not as if you actually do anything apart from just sit there, so why should it take so much out of you? But it does.

The split second I woke, I knew something was wrong.

The ceiling above my head was not my ceiling. I shot bolt upright. It got worse. This wasn't my cot. I leapt to my feet. Unfortunately, I leapt too quickly, went all wibbly and toppled forward. Sticking my arm out to break my fall, I misjudged the precise position of the cot bars, and my outstretched arm plunged through the gap between them. My head, which in cases like this seems to have the unerring knack of finding just what it is that my hand missed, zeroed in on the bars. And in that briefest of brief interludes between realising my head was going to whack into something very solid and when it actually happened, a thought occurred to me:

'This is going to hurt.'

And I was right.

I opened my mouth wide and let rip. Smooth shot into the room. In no time at all I was in her arms and she was rubbing my back. (What is it with all this back rubbing?) Smooth tried her best but I was inconsolable. Moments later Hairy appeared carrying a bag. He opened it and out came Teddy Bear, Piggy and Steve the Rabbit. I pulled them towards me and held them close. And as I hung on to my friends, my sobs subsided.

But their comforting presence seemed to highlight the larger, sadder truth. They were only three out of so many. Would I ever see the others again? That night I hardly slept at all. Neither did Hairy or Smooth. Obviously they shared my misgivings.

Some holiday this was going to be.

# The Endless Sandpit

The beach is a sandpit that goes on forever. On my trek to find if someone had hidden the end of it, I passed all manner of Hairies and Smooths. Almost all of them were wearing little more than an incredibly snuggly-fitting nappy. These were so skimpy that I seriously doubted they could possibly serve the primary purpose of a nappy. What they did do, however, is to reveal just how hairy Hairies are and just how smooth Smooths are. And maybe this was the purpose of these pseudo-nappies. Maybe their whole point was to emphasise the differences. Even to boast about them.

Anyway, by the time I got back to base camp, I was ready for a bit of a play in the sand. If you haven't done it for a while, you should. It really is one of life's simple pleasures.

But as I played with the sand, what struck me was that it was subtly different to your normal, run-of-the-mill sandpit sand. The grains were bigger, rougher and grittier. But the touch of it on my fingers, the feel of it under my feet, though at first unexpected, soon became an unalloyed joy. Somehow this sand, with its coarse, rough and ready nature, was sand more at ease with itself, sand less buttoned up, sand sans all pretensions.

In no time at all, the sand's happy-go-lucky demeanour proved infectious. I felt freer, more joyful, devoid of all concerns. The world was my sandpit. And my sandpit went on forever.

# The Sea, The Sea

I know not the words, nor have sufficient skill with the words that I do have, to do justice to what I felt when I first encountered the sea.

It was like coming home.

Maybe that's why whenever I caught sight of it I would head off, full pelt, like a newly hatched turtle answering an irresistible call. I don't know. All I do know is that I loved it.

It was wet, it was big, and it was mine.

As I stared, in awe, at the unbelievable sight I resolved never to forget what I was feeling at that precise moment. So every time I saw the sea it would be like the first time.

And when the ice cold water lapped over my feet it was like being anointed. That day I promised the sea I would never forget it. And that I would return as often as I could.

# The Ice Cream Man Cometh

When I first tried it, I didn't like it. It was so odd, so perplexing and so damned cold. I never knew that anything could be that cold. It was so cold that as I bit into it, it bit back. Furthermore, I couldn't figure out if it was a solid or a liquid. It looked like a solid but in many ways acted like a liquid. For instance, when I reached out to touch it my hand went straight in. And when it bit me, my hand came straight out too. All in all my first encounter with ice cream was not a resounding success.

The second time I tried it, however, I loved it. It was, and I use this word advisedly, sensational. Even the fact that, after I had devoured this liquid-solid ice-cold conundrum, it left a slowly warming, sticky residue of juice around my face was a cause for rejoicing. Indeed, since then I have always endeavoured to smear a fair amount of the stuff all around the environs of my mouth. Getting the ice cream 'everywhere' has become integral, if not compulsory, to the whole ice-cream experience.

Since my conversion from complete sceptic to evangelical believer I have pondered long and hard on the issue of ice cream to see if I can ascertain the precise nature of its undoubted power. The closest I come to explaining the phenomenon can be summed up in one word: frisson. My theory therefore is:

Ice cream is a frisson made solid. Or liquid. (Or both.) And edible.

Is it any wonder I'm hooked on the stuff?

# Where Sea And Sand Do Battle

There is some kind of dispute going on between the sea and the sand. It is a slow war of attrition waged on a seemingly unending front that exists wherever the two meet. What is at stake is whether an area of space between the two foes is going to be occupied by sea or sand.

Why the two adversaries fell out in the first place, I have no idea. But as I watched the battle I got the impression that the fray had been going on for quite some time. I must also admit my loyalties were somewhat divided. Even though I had only recently met the pair, I had developed a friendship with each that I could see stretching far into the future.

It's hard to know who originally held the territory in question, but the conflict played out in the following manner. First the sand claimed the space, essentially by just occupying it. Then the sea staked its claim by rushing in and covering the sand. Then the sand re-asserted itself and pushed the sea back. Then the whole sequence would be repeated.

Thinking that maybe I could do something to mediate between the two adversaries, I sat myself down right on the front line and tried to talk to them both. Oh, the arrogance of youth. They ignored me and got on with their dispute. I got more agitated. I grabbed a handful of sand. I splashed my other hand down on the incoming sea. But they weren't paying me any attention. They weren't rude, they were just pre-occupied. So in the end I let them get on with it.

I began to notice that even though a conflict was definitely being acted out, in many ways it was quite good-natured. The moves and counter-moves seemed so repetitive that they possessed an almost ritualistic element. Sand and sea were like two duellists locked in a never-ending fight that both had long ago realised neither could win. They had come to a mutual agreement. They would fight, but they wouldn't try too hard.

Later I realised that if I was to draw any lesson from the dispute between the sand and the sea it is that sometimes in life you can agree to disagree. To do so is neither a defeat nor a victory, it's just pragmatic. And pragmatism was invented so that we could get on with the things we really want to do.

# Strange Horses Going Nowhere

They live by the sea. They live between the sea and the buildings. They live in a circular hut without walls. They are unlike any horses I have ever known. Their eyes stare out, their lips curl back, and they are every colour you could ever imagine.

As Hairy pushed the buggy towards them, the most incredible thing happened. Music filled the air, then the horses started to jump up and down. And forward. I slumped in my buggy and tried to take in the full splendour of the sight. All too soon it came to an end. The music stopped. The horses stopped dancing.

And then, and then, and then, Hairy lifted me in his arms, carried me toward the wondrous beasts and perched me on the back of one of them. I leant forward on the horse and laid my cheek against its body. It was cold and hard and strong. Hairy lifted me upright again and gave me a soft strap to hold, then clambered up behind me, his arms around my body.

The music started again. Tentatively the horse swayed upwards. I rose with mine. Together we moved up and forward and down. The world glided by in a blur of colour and confusion. Excitement surged through me. So much excitement that I had to scream to let it out.

We travelled, bizarrely, through a world that kept repeating itself. The same buildings, the same cars, the same sea, kept coming into view again and again and again. But I was too caught up in the moment to ponder long on this issue. It was a bit like being in a swing — but different. It was a bit like being on a slide — but different. And it was a bit like being in a car — but different. Then the music and the horse stopped. Hairy climbed down and lifted me from the creature's back. Holding me, he walked away from the horse's hut, then turned back so that I could see them again. As I watched, the music started and the horses set off once more. I stared transfixed and tried to make sense of it all. But it was all too much.

Later that night, as I lay in the strange cot, I got to thinking. When I got past reliving the sheer physical thrill of it all, I started to ponder on the journey that the horse and I had been on. What occurred to me was this: we had gone nowhere. We had gone round in a circle. Then another. Then another circle. When I got off I was back where I had started. Yet the journey itself had been stupendous.

I sucked contemplatively on my dummy and reflected. By now sleep had put in an appearance and was edging its way over to me. I threw Teddy Bear at it, but it kept on coming. I picked up my blanket and tipped that over the side of the cot hoping to trip sleep up and delay it for a while. All to no avail. Now sleep had slipped into the cot itself. I backed away and squashed myself against the bars. I even managed to squidge half my body into the narrow crack between the edge of the mattress and the side of the cot. But sleep kept coming. In desperation I shouted at sleep as loud as I could. Sleep hesitated for an instant. And in that instant an explanation, of sorts, came to me for what I had been through with the horse.

Maybe, just maybe, sometimes the journey is more important than the destination.

# Would We All Get On Better If We Played In Bigger Sandpits?

What really convinced me of the glorious potency of the sand in the endless sandpit was the effect it had on Hairy and Smooth. On those predominantly glum, frequently annoying, and all too often angry purveyors of seriously negative vibes through their repeated use of that 'N' word, it was a revelation. They lightened up. They let me get on with things. They even tried playing themselves. Now, I'm not saying they were any good at it, but at least they had a go. Hairy commandeered the spade that I was happily waving around in front of my face trying to see what happens when you push the air out of the way and whether anything rushes in to fill its place, and started using it to fill the bucket up with sand. I've no idea why. But he seemed intent on the task. So, not wanting to disappoint him, I feigned interest.

Actually, after the first couple of shovelfuls hit the bottom of the bucket it was quite boring. But, to my credit, I stuck with it. Hairy was so into what he was doing, it obviously meant a lot to him. Eventually, after what seemed like yonks, the bucket was completely full. Hairy took the spade and patted down the sand with it so that the sand compacted and its surface was smooth. It wasn't the most exciting of manoeuvres, but by the intensity Hairy's exhortations to me I figured he thought it was important that I pay particular attention. So I did. (Or, at least I pretended to.)

However, what he did next immediately seized my wavering attention. In one swift move he turned the bucket upside down. Then he lifted the bucket away, but the sand remained in the shape of the missing bucket. It was an outrage. I knocked over the sand-bucket abomination in disgust. Well, to be honest, in disgust and delight because knocking it over was a lot of fun. My main point, however, was that this in no way was the right state for sand to be in. Sand, especially the sand in this endless sandpit, is a free spirit. It's meant to lounge around and do nothing. It's meant to be thrown, in a cavalier fashion, through the air. It's meant to be secretly ferreted in the nooks and crannies of your clothes only to be set free much later at home. It is not meant to conform to any rigid structure. That's why I knocked the monstrosity down.

But Hairy built another one. So I knocked that down too. And another one. And another one. By now, what had started out on my part as a protest had become little more than a demolition fest. All thought of social justice had been pushed to the recesses of my mind. I was doing what I was doing because it was fun. So was Hairy. Smooth was watching and smiling, too. I blame the sand. It makes you do senseless things. And enjoy them.

It was while H and S were indulging in spot of walrus work (just lying on the sand) that I headed off on another of my treks and came to some major conclusions. What I noted was that in the endless sandpit the usual rules of sandpit interaction seem to be suspended. Conflict, if it does occur, happens at an altogether lower level. And disputes seem to be rapidly resolved.

In your conventional, everyday sandpit, every step you take, every move you make, is designed to establish your pre-eminence in the hierarchy. In the endless sandpit hierarchies don't seem to apply. All the normal rules of social interaction have decided to take a day off. You can mix and play with people whom, in ordinary life, you would compete with or avoid. You can share your bucket and spade and not have this taken as a sign of weakness or deferment.

It is all most odd. But very enjoyable. Needless to say, I spent some time trying to analyse just why, precisely, the Endless Sandpit had the makings of an embryonic utopian society. At first it was the powerful, liberating effect of the sand that seemed to hold the key. But what I concluded is that it's all to do with territory. In your conventional sandpit space is limited so one must compete to ensure one gets enough space to do what one needs to do. Naturally in competing, a hierarchy develops.

But what happens if space isn't limited? What happens when the sandpit goes on forever? Well, there's no need to compete. No order or hierarchy need develop. It's an analysis that leads to an obvious, and I believe very profound, question.

Wouldn't the world be a much better place if only we had bigger sandpits?

# That Old Departure Lounge Feeling

**L**et me share with you the titles of some of the other fascinating holiday reflections that I considered including in this work:

Seagulls. Do They Ever Shut Up?

Fish, Chips And Tomato Ketchup. There Is A God.

Has Hairy Always Looked Like That Under His Clothes?

Is Candy Floss What All Clouds Taste Of?

Here Be Monsters. Official.

However, few things are as boring as someone banging on and on about their holiday so I may get back to them in another book. Or not.

# MONTH XIX

Oh well, back to the daily grind.

# The Swing Thing. Towards An Understanding Of The Addictive Qualities Of Motion

S mooth. Ground (backwards). Hang in the air. Ground (forwards). Smooth. Sky (forwards). Hang in the air. Sky (backwards). Smooth.

Repeat.

Increase speed.

Written down it doesn't sound like much, does it? But when you're doing it, when you're swinging, it's total, it's full on, it's both barrels, it's the complete enchilada and, as Johnny Rotten once put it, 'we mean it maaaaan!'

To be honest, I don't really understand why it is such a blast, I only know that it is. So overwhelming an experience is it, that the second I see a swing the alarm bells start ringing. Not alarm bells warning of something alarming, but alarm bells heralding the imminent arrival of something wonderful.

At this point Smooth sometimes tries to distract me with some of the lesser, make-weight attractions of the play park. Some of these have a few good points (e.g. trying to get off a moving roundabout is always a good way to test S's response time). But who is she kidding? In the play park, the swing's the thing.

So you approach the swing. Your heart pounds. Your hands go clammy. Your feet almost trip over themselves in excitement. Then Smooth hoists you skywards and deposits you in the cockpit of your very own chariot of the air.

Unless, of course, there's a queue. Then you're caught in that seemingly endless departure lounge, with a flight delay of who knows how long, surrounded by disgruntled individuals, and nothing to do but press your nose to the glass and watch other people jet off. Before long you hate everyone and everything and can't imagine why you came in the first place. You vow never to come again. So you shout a little. You scream a little. You might even, in a moment of madness, rush towards one of the swings determined to hijack the thing. My advice is chill out and try the philosophical approach. No one can hog a swing forever. (As Mrs Thatcher found out much to her surprise.)

Eventually someone, somewhere, gets off. Then you're in, you're on and you're swinging. Is it the rush of air that hurtles past your face that is the key to it all? Is it the constantly changing vista? Is it the thrill of flying and falling, falling and flying? In truth, when you're up there you're so living in the moment that rational analysis is the last thing on your mind. You're so alive, so firmly caught up in the immediacy of it all, that you don't have time to think. You don't want to think. You just want to be. Maybe that's the secret. Maybe being on a swing is all about being alive.

No wonder it's addictive.

# Sharing. Resistance Is Futile,
# But We All Must Resist

Possession, it has been said, is nine tenths of the law. Well, just walk a mile in my bootees and you'll find a very different state of affairs prevails. What's mine may very well be my own, but all too often it's someone else's too. Especially if Hairy or Smooth are on the case.

I'll illustrate my argument by harking back to an incident that happened just the other day. I was sitting in my room merrily playing with a pushy toy that I knew for a fact was mine, when in came Smooth. She was not alone. With her was an individual of similar stature to myself. For the sake of this anecdote (and on the advice of my lawyer), I shall call this individual 'Birdbath'.

At first, things went well. I looked at Birdbath. Birdbath looked at me. I looked back. Birdbath started to cry. Fool that I was I took this to mean that I had won the decisive first round, had clearly established certain criteria and laid down a hierarchy. To be blunt, I thought I had proved that I was in charge. When Birdbath went on to bury a very blubbing face just above Smooth's knees I thought my victory was complete.

I turned back to my pushy toy and busied myself with some fairly impressive pushy work. As I went about my business, I could hear in the background Smooth trying to placate the still whimpering Birdbath. I paid little heed.

Then the whimpering stopped. I looked up and saw Birdbath approaching. Smooth watched apprehensively.

What happened next beggars belief. Birdbath took the pushy toy from me. I, naturally, took it back. Birdbath burst into tears. Then Smooth came up, removed the pushy toy from my grasp, and handed it to Birdbath. To make it worse, she mouthed the cursed word 'share' and gave me a load of garbage about having plenty of other toys to play with.

Not wanting to dwell too long on the blindingly obvious injustice of this course of events, let me just point out three things.

1 It was my toy.

2 I was playing with it.

3 Yes, I have got lots of other toys so why doesn't Birdbath play with one of those?

Sorry, let me point out four things.

4 What kind of stupid name is 'Birdbath' anyway?

(Okay, I admit that this last point is a cheap shot given the fact that I chose the name, but I was annoyed.)

Despite my outrage, I paused, collected my thoughts and tried to present a reasoned argument as to why, in light of the overwhelming body of evidence in my favour, Smooth may have made a slight error of judgement. Unfortunately, my still rudimentary grasp of oratorical skills somewhat hampered my advocacy, and I was reduced to trying to advance my case by tugging on the leg of Smooth's trousers and shrieking. This had no effect.

So I did what any red-blooded person would do in the circumstances. I took back what was rightfully mine.

Smooth went ballistic. She picked me up. Removed the

pushy toy from my hands. Gave it to Birdbath. Then she removed me from the room. Let me spell that out for you in more detail: she removed me from my own room. It was as if I was the one in the wrong.

Justice is not a nebulous concept. It can't be stretched or bent for the sake of convenience. Things are either right or wrong. So what on earth was all this about?

When I had time to sit back and analyse the situation, the meaning became clear. I realised it was nothing to do with Birdbath. Birdbath was an unwitting prawn in the game. You see, it was all about power. What Smooth was doing was demonstrating to me that she had the power and I did not. And if you have enough power, you can subvert justice and define it how you will.

It was a harsh lesson, but one worth learning. Never, ever forget that the personal is always political.

# Regrets, I've Had A Few

A large tub of nappy cream. A loose lid. Hairy out of the room. Who wouldn't be tempted?

Look, I'm not saying I'm proud of what I did. All I'm saying is I did what I did. It's not a question of right and wrong. Of course, I know what I did was 'wrong'. But what kind of person would I be if I hadn't done it? And, in a funny way, isn't breaking the rules just a way of validating the fact that rules exist? (Okay, I admit that is a pretty ropy piece of post-rationalising justification, but it was worth a shot.)

If I'm honest, however, as I slathered the walls in nappy cream, as I rubbed it into my hair, as I flicked it hither and thither (and yon) watching it flop onto and into the carpet in abstract splashes of oleaginous gloop, as I gloried in the squidginess of a handful of the stuff squeezed between the slipperiest of fingers, rational justification was the last thing on my mind. Because I was in the moment, I was of the moment, I was the moment.

Wasn't it Stevie Winwood in 'Higher Love' who sang 'If you see a chance, take it'. An admirable philosophy, I think you'll agree.

An early bath is a small price to pay.

# The Shame, The Shame

It's the sheer indignity of it all that gets me. The sheer indignity and the embarrassment. And the utter, utter, utter public humiliation.

There I was merrily minding my own business, doing my own thing, when Smooth swooped into action. I was helping someone, who was a bit bigger than me, with the game they were playing, namely piling bricks on top of one another to create a structure that although lacking aesthetic merit, more than made up for it in height. I was helping by periodically knocking the bricks over. The bigger person obviously enjoyed my participation because each time I intervened they got more and more excited. Indeed, after my last little shove the person was so happy they had tears of joy welling up.

In short, we were getting on like a house on fire. (Incidentally, why is it good to get on like 'a house on fire'? Surely 'a house on fire' is a very bad thing?) Anyway, it was at this point, totally out of the blue, that I found myself ripped from my revelry and hoisted upwards towards the hell of social disgrace that Smooth had decided for her own nefarious means to inflict upon me.

Let me talk you through the complete incident. First Smooth brings me up to her face. Then her nose kind of crinkles up. Then she utters some utter banality and feigns a look of concern. And then – I advise you to look away now if you're of nervous disposition – and then, in full view of the surrounding masses, she spins me round, lifts me a little higher, and sniffs my bottom.

Humiliation swept over me like bubbly bath water.

Then it went from bad to worse. In fact, it motored straight past worse, put its foot down on the pedal and sped, cackling, into worser.

I was laid on the floor. My nether garments were brusquely removed. My derrière was exposed to the elements. My efforts were scooped up unceremoniously. A cursory wipe, a slapdash slathering of ice-cold cream, a fresh nappy applied, and my clothing shoddily replaced. All in full public view. And it's not as if this were a one-off. It happens time and time and time again. Someone should do something. But no one ever does.

I blame the government.

# Nursery Crimes Six.
# Utopia in the Sheep Pen

'Baa-baa black sheep have you any wool?
Yes sir, yes sir, three bags full.
One for the master, one for the dame,
And one for the little boy who lives down the lane'

A cursory examination of this rhyme may lead the inexperienced student to characterise the piece as nothing more than a blatant apologia for a wholly questionable social structure in which there are 'masters', 'dames' and 'little boys who live down the lane'. The 'little boys' being representative of the working class or underclass of rural poor. But the inexperienced student would be wrong.

Delving a little deeper reveals an altogether more utopian model.

The initial question, for instance, implies that the sheep is not merely a mindless agricultural labourer ripe for exploitation. It implies that the questioner is not seeking to roughly and unexpectedly shear the wool from the unsuspecting sheep, but is politely enquiring about it and may have an innate understanding about the technical skill and emotional aspects of producing wool. This suggests that the questioner sees the sheep as on an equal footing to themselves. (Or should that be equal hoofing?)

The sheep's reply, with its use of 'yes sir', could imply a degree of deference, but it may possibly be that the sheep, having been treated with respect, is merely returning the courtesy. Reference to 'three bags' may be boastful, but let that pass.

Moving on, isn't allocation of one bag each for the master, dame, and little boy clearly a reference to a society that, although having a distinct hierarchy, also boasts a strongly egalitarian element in as much as every individual involved gets exactly the same amount of wool?

Then there is the matter of the character at the centre of the whole affair. Baa-baa black sheep herself. Elsewhere in literature, and indeed in our society itself, black sheep get a uniformly bad press. They are derided and vilified and I would go so far as to say, demonised. But not in this piece. Here, I would argue, the black sheep is very much the heroine. No reference is made to the issue of 'black sheepness'. Here we have a story about a sheep who happens to be black, not a story about a 'black sheep'. And we have a society not trapped and held back with the negative stereotypes usually, and in my view erroneously, associated with the 'blackness' of black sheep.

That's why I warm to this rhyme immensely. Now where's that rusk I filed under the sofa cushions for future use?

# How To Keep The Opposition Off Balance

Revert to crawling occasionally.

# I Am A Teenage Crisp Addict

**W**as it that first crunch that got me hooked? Was it the sharp salt tang that ricocheted around my mouth? Was it the way that the whole brittle structure dissolved away to nothing on my tongue? Or was it just the glorious crinkliness of the packet?

I don't really care. Whether it was one of these factors, or all of them, or something else entirely, doesn't really matter. All that matters is that from the very first instant a crisp alighted in my mouth, I was hooked.

If the raison d'être of ordinary foods is nourishment, then the point of a crisp is sensation. The crisp is very much the Andy Warhol of the food world. It's about surface, it's about texture, it's about instant, overwhelming gratification. And, I'm sorry to say, it's about addiction.

No matter how crowded the room I'm in, no matter how noisy the park is, no matter how surreptitiously the deed is done, if a packet of crisps is opened anywhere within a eight-kilometre radius of me, I hear the joyous sound. It calls to me like the Sirens of ancient Greece luring unsuspecting sailors to their doom. Once I've heard the call, I am powerless to resist.

I have wriggled free from the grasp of Smooth, I have stomped straight through the muddiest of puddles, I have clambered over furniture, I have shoved aside the diddiest of people, all because I have to get to the crisps. What's more, I have no regard for the crisps' legal owner. I see crisps anywhere, in the hands of anyone, and I know that I must make them mine. And make them mine now.

When I'm being kind to myself, I look at my actions and think that the strength of my response is so great that it must be the consequence of a fundamental natural urge. The urge to eat crisps must be akin to the urge to breathe, or to sleep, or to throw toys from your buggy.

When I'm being less kind to myself, or maybe just more objective, I face up to the harsh reality that my addiction is my fault. I am addicted because I choose to be. I am addicted because I am weak, weak, weak. And if I just had enough willpower I could break the vice-like grip of my sordid habit.

It's not as if I haven't tried to get away from The Call Of The Crisp. Time and time again I have stiffened my resolve. Time and time again I have told myself to 'Just Say No'. And time and time again, I have fallen at the very first hurdle. On occasion so great has my craving been that I have found myself snatching empty crisp packets from the street, ripping them open and licking the dregs from their very corners. When you're in the grips of an addiction you know no shame.

I can but hope is that as I grow older I learn to curb my grubby desires. Or at least learn to indulge them with a touch more discretion. For the moment all I can say is, and I say it with no pride, I am a teenage crisp addict. (Teenage month-wise, that is).

# Babysitters

ere's a conundrum. We live in a supposedly objective world, but we can only perceive it via subjective senses. What got me thinking about all this was the matter of babysitters. Babysitters, like the owl, the badger and the slow loris, are nocturnal creatures. Babysitters take the place of parents when your parents have got bored with you. Babysitters tend to be Smooth-like in appearance.

Beyond these simple facets of babysitters, I used to think that they could be divided up into two distinct categories. There were babysitters who were lovable and there were the babysitters who were loathable. Then the other night I came across a babysitter who had always been ensconced in the lovable camp and discovered that she was now loathable. Why?

I pondered long and hard on the matter. The answer, when it came, landed me firmly in the objective world - subjective senses debate. You see what I figured out was that it wasn't her who had changed, it was me.

All of which led me to my revised model of babysitter types. The revised model goes something like this: there are two types of babysitter and it all depends on your state of mind.

The first type of babysitter I will call The Understudy. The Understudy is how a babysitter will seem to you if, when you encounter them for the first time, you are in a bad mood. Hence you will bawl, you will shout and you will scream. Everything The Understudy tries to do will make you feel unhappy, unloved and somehow cheated.

The parallel that is relevant here is to imagine yourself on a trip to the theatre to see a play it's been almost impossible to get tickets for, starring one of the true greats of the stage. For example, anything with the incandescent Dame Judi Dench in it (or Zoë Wanamaker). You've hacked your way through the milling Saturday night crowds. You've bought one of those programmes that are quite expensive given that there's hardly anything in them and that you'll never look at again once you go home and will eventually find yourself trying to decide whether you want to hang onto it seven years later when you're moving house and when you do decide you do want to hang onto it your partner will look at you as if to say 'I thought we were supposed to be throwing things out' but you'll ignore them anyway and keep the programme knowing full well that the next time you will look at the programme again will be another seven years down the line when you're moving out of the new house but by now the programme has come to symbolise a tiny act of rebellion in which you try to maintain some degree of individuality within a relationship that, even though it is a loving one, can be a bit stifling at times. You've bought a drink. You've been appalled at the price of the drink. You've been unable to enjoy the drink because, with every expensive sip, you can't get out of your head the thought that you could have got a decent bottle of wine for the same money and wouldn't have had to swig it back in an overcrowded, overheated bar. Then you go and sit down in your seat and all these petty niggles fly away because you are about to watch the glory that is Dame Judi Dench (or Zoë Wanamaker). Then a voice comes over the public address system and tells you that due to unforeseen circumstances Dame Judi Dench (or Zoë Wanamaker) can't perform tonight and her part will be taken by Evadne Shrub – The Understudy.

That's what it feels like when you wake up in a bad mood only to find a babysitter there. Is it any wonder that you kick up a fuss?

The second type of babysitter I will call the Supply/Substitute Parent. As the name suggests the Supply/Substitute Parent is akin to the supply/substitute teachers you get at school when your usual teacher is off sick. The Supply/Substitute Parent is how a babysitter will appear to you if you're in a good mood when you first come across them.

What will occur to your cunning little mind as you view this metaphorical lamb ripe for the slaughter, is that they don't know the rules. For example, The Supply/Substitute Parent simply doesn't know what time you go to bed. Or, and here's the great bit, even if they do know, you can easily talk them out of it. That's because, fundamentally, deep down, and in a way that makes them oh so easy to manipulate, all they really want is a quiet life. So, do a little crying, throw in a bit of running away work, spice it up with a soupcon of pouting, and the Supply/Substitute Parent will soon be like porridge in your hands.

All you have to do is let them play with the television and

the telephone and they'll let you get on with pretty much whatever you want. It can really be a most magical time.

The only finesse I suggest you add to these adventures is to try and make sure that just before you think that Hairy and Smooth are about to return, you take your foot off the gas and crash out in as cute a bodily arrangement as you can manage. This way Hairy and Smooth will think you've been an angel all night and they'll get the same poor sap to stand in for them again.

There you have the two basic types of babysitter. And like I said before which type you encounter all depends on the mood you're in when you encounter them. And as I also said before, it all goes to show that although we live in an objective world, we can only perceive it via subjective senses. And a subjective mind.

But that's only my opinion. A most objective opinion, I think you'll agree.

# MONTH XX

Churchill said 'jaw-jaw is better than war-war'.
But what if you can't speak?

# The Baby Monitor Wars. How It All Began

**M**y room is bugged. Yes, you heard me right, my room is bugged. I was merrily pulling my Telletubbies posters off my wall to see if there was a safe behind one of them when I spied (an appropriate choice of word as you will see) a small red dot of light lurking between the toys on one of the shelves. So I investigated. What I discovered, I'm afraid to say, can only be described as a listening device.

It is an outrage. It is a scandal. It is a clear violation of my human rights. It is a complete negation of the trust that was finally taking root between me and the people I had at last begun to stop thinking of as my captors.

All I can say is that all bets are off and I am removing my negotiators from the conference table. I'm sorry, but if we can't proceed on a basis of trust, what hope is there?

I am entering a phase of active, non-violent, non-co-operation. I am embarking on a campaign of civil disobedience. I am, in short, making a stand. I will report back to you on how it goes.

# The Baby Monitor Wars. Phase I.
# The Hunger Strike.

I haven't eaten anything for two whole days. It's got them rattled. At first they just shrugged it off. But as each meal time passed and I still refused food, they began to look perturbed. They tried everything. But I was having none of it. No books, no games, no pleading, no nothing was going to distract me from my course of action.

Boy, you should have seen the floor around the high chair. I was whacking proffered spoons away like the mighty Viv Richards in his prime, with such regularity that it couldn't be long before the EU would have to come in, peruse the foothills of food gathering around my chair, and declare that we had an official gloop mountain on our hands.

The turning point came towards the end of Day Two. It was a ploy so sneaky that despite my utter contempt for my adversaries, I had to admire their ingenuity. The food got better. The perennial procession of gloop, goo and sludge changed. At long last there was stuff you could recognise. At long last there was stuff that smelled vaguely appealing. At long last there was stuff that made you want to eat it.

But I held firm. I refused to let even a single morsel cross the threshold of my mouth. I was, even if I say so myself, heroic in my resolve. There was, however, one problem.

I was really hungry.

# The Baby Monitor Wars. Phase II.
# The Struggle Continues

Conventional wisdom would tell you that David had no chance against Goliath. It would advise you that the Vietcong had no hope of beating the US. It would say that Arthur Ashe should have been trounced by Jimmy Connors in '75. History, however, tells us different.

It's all about belief in yourself. You may not have the physical firepower to out gun them, but you may have the mental fire power to out think them. I had to duck and dive. I had to hit and run. I had to wage what I hoped would be a classic among the annals of guerrilla war.

So I did. My next sortie took my foe totally by surprise. I refused to wear the clothes they gave me.

My logic was that I was a political prisoner, involved in a political dispute, and so should be accorded the right to choose my own clothes. Of course, this was but a pretext. My refusal to don the clothes of the oppressor was just a way of widening the dispute and creating another arena of conflict. But, if you want to take it on a more philosophical level, it could be seen as a cri de coeur with me shouting (metaphorically) 'I am not your dolly. You can't dress me how you will. I don't care how cute I look. And I'm not here just so that your friends can come round and admire your latest purchases from Baby Gap. Even if they do have some really great stuff.' (Okay, so that last bit about Baby Gap isn't the most politically profound piece of liberation theology in the world, but you get my drift.)

The details of the struggle are immaterial. Actually, on second thoughts, they were completely 'material'. Because it was a struggle about 'material'. The material that clothes are made of. (Or should that be 'of which clothes are made'? Hold on, I am writing of my time as a revolutionary freedom fighter, so surely I should reject all petit bourgeois rules of grammar as nothing more than the clanking chains with which the ruling ideologically bankrupt junta enforce the suppression of our means of expression and so, in a very real sense, suppress the hopes and aspirations of generation after generation of the dispossessed?) (Gosh, all this revolution malarkey can be heady stuff when you're young.)

(I wonder if I'm beginning to use brackets too much?)

I won't go into details of how I refused the clothes of the oppressor. Let's just say that I did. And let's just say that on many occasions there were tears before bedtime.

Of course, in the end I was always made to wear the hated garments. But Hairy and Smooth had to resort to the use of such overwhelming force that I'm pretty certain they knew that the moral victory was mine. As I stood there, proud and defiant in my cot, the clothes took on a highly charged and symbolic nature. In much the same way that Gandhi, in his struggle to free the people of the Indian subcontinent from colonial rule, had rejected cloth made in England in favour of home-spun material, I had made my point.

And, as the long days of defiance led into the restless hit-and-run of night-time disturbances, the old saying of my people proved once again to be true: 'You can put a person in a sleepy suit, but you can't make them sleep'.

# The Baby Monitor Wars. Phase III.
## The Writing's On The Wall

I begin writing on the wall. The authorities, in a typical jack-booted knee jerk reaction, confiscate all my writing material. Further evidence that there's nothing dictators fear more than free expression.

I resolve to learn to get onto the Internet at the earliest possible opportunity.

# The Baby Monitor Wars. Phase IV.
# It Was All A Mistake

**B**oy, do I feel foolish. The bug, the listening device, the snake in the grass, the Judas at the last supper, the teacher's pet in the classroom, the snout, the copper's narc, the whistleblower, the canary, the electronic informer, the call-it-what-you-will, well, it was nothing of the kind. I had totally got the wrong end of the stick. I was looking at things through the fat end of the binoculars. I was eating the packet and not the crisps.

That thing on the shelf that I had taken as a device planted by Hairy and Smooth to check up on me and to keep me under control was, in fact, completely the opposite. It was the means for me to check up on them. It was a way for me to keep them under control.

I don't know why I hadn't figured it out before. I had taken the fact that they could hear what I was up to at any time to mean that they had me in their power. However, just look at how the system actually works in practice. If I'm busy getting on with my own thing, no-one bothers me. But if I shout, someone comes. Indeed, if I shout really loud and spice it up with a sprinkling of sobs, screams or choking noises, someone comes running.

The phrase 'beck and call' comes to mind.

You don't have to be the tallest castle in the sandpit in order to figure out how to work this system to your advantage. So I did.

I've called off The Struggle. Hairy and Smooth seem mightily, mightily relieved. They can't understand why the hostilities have ceased. But they are grateful. They were on the verge of defeat. I think that if I'd just pushed on with one final offensive it wouldn't have been long before the helicopters were landing on the roof of the embassy and the diplomats were scrabbling to get on. And to think it was all for a simple misunderstanding.

Still, I learned some useful techniques. And you never know when things like that might come in handy.

# Other Buggies, Other Lives

You know when you're on a train trundling through the suburbs and you're bored with the book you brought, and wishing you had bought that copy of *Hello!* on the station platform and so what if people think you're shallow, and you can't be bothered to totter through the carriages to get a plastic cup of that tepid dishwater they have the cheek to call coffee, and you wonder why that bloke with his mobile has to talk so loud as if whoever he's talking to is interested in the fact that he's 'on the train!' let alone the rest of you in the carriage, so in desperation you turn and peer through the grime-stained windows at the gardens of the houses that back onto the tracks, and then for nothing more than a fleeting instant you catch sight of the lighted interior of a room, and suddenly you find yourself riveted?

That's what it's like.

That's why other people's buggies are endlessly fascinating. It's not the buggies in themselves that engage the mind. (Although, it must be said that some of the designs are pretty interesting. And some of them are pretty absurd. There's that bizarre, low-slung hammock affair that gets propelled around on three large, all-terrain wheels that looks like a land yacht with the sails blown away. I mean, what's all that about? It's like owning a massive four-wheel drive off-roader just so that you can pop along to the supermarket to get a couple of brioches. Boy do I feel sorry for anyone stuck in one of those contraptions. But I'm getting off the point. Sorry.) It's what the buggies tell you that intrigues. It's what they reveal that pulls you to them.

It all begins when you spot an empty buggy. You have to get to it, and stake your claim before anyone else does. Then the fun can really begin. I always start with the straps. My purpose is entirely practical. I'm convinced that if I study enough straps for long enough, I'm going to eventually figure out how to undo the damn things. If Hairy and Smooth can do it, then just how difficult can it be?

When I've had my fill of fiddling about with the straps, I move on to an inch-by-inch, almost forensic, search of the buggy seat. It is within the confines and environs of the buggy seat that morsels of food get inadvertently trapped like stricken vessels caught up in the Bermuda Triangle. And just as historians of today like nothing better than digging around in the rubbish dumps of yesteryear in order to ascertain how life was lived way back when, I like to collect and collate data on fallen foods as a way of getting a very real feel of how the buggy proprietor lives their life.

And you can eat what you find.

Crisps of all denominations feature heavily, as do raisins, crushed biscuits, squashed sandwiches and mashed banana. Sometimes two or more can combine into Ferrero Rocher-esque trufflette of delights. But even if all your foraging reveals is a single, fluff-encrusted raisin, you're still coming out ahead. So enjoy.

Then it's time to check out the accessories. These are the things that have been added to the basic buggy spec in order to upgrade and improve the whole in-buggy experience. They include strapped-on books, strapped-on toys, trays, umbrellas, and occasional tied-on balloons. It's a generally acknowledged rule that the number of accessories attached to any buggy is inversely proportional to the amount of time the buggy proprietor will want to spend in it. Pursuing my studies via discussions with said proprietors, I have discovered a most intriguing anomaly. Buggies festooned with excess accessories are owned by individuals with what can be best described as short attention spans. The Hairies and Smooths belonging to these individuals attempt to solve the problem by providing them with more and more things to distract their attention. I may be way out of line here, but surely what's needed is not more things, but fewer.

Accessories assessed, I move onto the mechanics of the thing. I examine the wheels, I test turning circles, I check out the steering, I try the brakes. If the brakes are firmly on I carry out a stability audit by employing the topple test. Last but not least, I investigate the suspension. This involves clambering up into the seat of the buggy and vigorously jumping up and down. A certain degree of caution needs to be exercised here. On several occasions this facet of my buggy MOT has unexpectedly turned into an inadvertent topple test.

Finally, it's time to delve into the under-buggy basket area. Under here, anything goes. I have encountered food, drink, books, clothes, toys, shoes, mobile phones, cigarettes, flowers, light electrical appliances, hats, and several magazines with George Clooney on the cover. It's a veritable goldmine of lifestyle choices. And it's after a shift in this particular goldmine that I tend to call a halt to my investigations. Then I sit back and ponder on all that I have discovered. And it's then that I indulge in a particular favourite pastime of mine. Match the owner to the buggy.

I invariably get it right. Except, of course, when I get it wrong.

# Leakage

**Shit happens.**

# It Seemed Like A Good Idea At The Time

I don't know why I hadn't thought of it before. It was the obvious answer to the age-old problem. It represented nothing less than a symbolic turning point on my road to true independence and individuality.

You see, the thing is, I was good at climbing. Climbing, to me, was a way I could increase my height without having to grow. Climbing was a way of accessing whole new worlds of opportunity. And climbing was a way of gaining some much-needed perspective on my environment. What, from ground level, is all too often a confusion of stuff competing for your attention becomes a comprehensible map of possibilities. And climbing is fun.

Now every morning I wake up and find myself in my cot. It's the norm. It's how things should be. However there are the bars. The bars keep you in. No matter how happy you may be to frolic within your cot post waking, there inevitably comes the time when you yearn for the world beyond the strictly defined boundaries of cotfordshire.

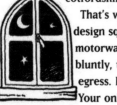

That's when the fundamental flaw in cot design squashes, like a hedgehog on a motorway, all hopes of freedom. Put bluntly, the cot does not allow for easy egress. It confines you; it imprisons you. Your only hope of reaching the visible world beyond is via the intervention of Hairy or Smooth.

You are reliant on them to release you from your bondage.

Or are you? A thought sidled into my head like a ticket tout approaching a punter. I grabbed it and ran with it.

I could climb out of the cot.

So I did.

And as I plummeted downwards I mused on the concept that falling is probably the exact opposite of climbing.

# How On Earth Does He Do Anything With That?

As I drank my milk this morning my spare hand rested in Hairy's hand. No doubt it has happened a hundred times before, but today for the first time I really looked at Hairy's hand. It is incredible. It is so big. How on earth he manages to do anything with it is a mystery. Yet it grips my hand so gently.

I slip my fingers from his grasp and slide my hand over his. I close my eyes and focus my mind on what I can feel. I feel roughness and ridges and warmth. I open my eyes again and look at his hand. I look at my hand. They are undoubtedly both the same thing, they are undoubtedly both hands, but they are so different.

My hands have been made by a master craftsman in the art of hand-making; his have been bodged together by some enthusiastic, but inexperienced novice. On the backs of the fingers there even sprout tufts of hair. Why? What possible use could it be?

I am overcome by a feeling of sadness. My hands are so perfect and unblemished; his are such a shoddy affair. I want to tell him that it doesn't matter, I want to tell him not to worry, I want to tell him that his hands are fine, but I can't.

That's because my mouth is fully occupied supping warm milk. And even if it wasn't, I haven't actually learned to talk yet.

All I can do is to carefully take one of his fingers in my hand and squeeze for all I'm worth. He looks down at me. He looks at my hand in his. He smiles. And gently squeezes back.

# What's Eating Them?

I am very much of the opinion that food and food procurement is one of the fundamentals of life. Food is something that I can both love and hate all in a very short space of time. The arena that the provision and consumption of food provides is also a space in which the key power relationships within my life can be played out. In short, food, for many reasons, is so much more than just food. Which is why I decided to step back from things for a while and tried to examine 'food' in a much broader context. What I discovered shocked me.

What I did was to shift the focus of my attention from my interactions with food (which had preoccupied me up until now) to those of Hairy and Smooth. I thought that if I checked out how they dealt with the food thing that maybe I could get a different handle on the whole shebang. I pretended to be doing nothing in particular, when all along I was making like David Attenborough that time he hung out with those gorillas. What I observed was deeply concerning.

Basically, Hairy and Smooth have appalling eating habits.

When I eat I sit at my usual table which is always reserved for me. I get comfortable, I settle myself in, maybe I have a bit of a play, and then I eat. Nothing particularly special in that. But, please note, I am sitting down when I eat. Call it what you will, comfort, common sense, good manners, etiquette even, it just seems the right way to go about things.

Hairy and Smooth, on the other hand, seem to do most of their eating standing up. And they bolt their food. They just cram it in, munch and swallow. It's almost as if they're too busy to eat properly. There is no savouring of the sensual pleasure of the food. And it's all over so quickly. Often they eat while doing other things. Hither and thither they will flit, biting, chewing, doing. Busy, busy, busy, busy. Is it any wonder that they not only do not enjoy their food, but they hardly seem to notice it at all.

It gets worse. Certain observations cause me to think that maybe one of the real problems is poverty. Hairy and Smooth are often reduced to eating the food that I leave behind. The other day, half way through a bowl of particularly unedifying gloop I decided I'd had enough, so I stopped eating and proceeded to see if I could break my own high-chair toy-putt record. When I looked over to see if Smooth was taking note of my endeavours, she was spooning up what was left in the bowl and polishing it off. I was shocked. But my shock soon turned to sadness. The only explanation I could come up with was poverty. Why else would Smooth eat my leftovers? I searched through the rapidly filling toy box that is my memory to see if it had always been like this. And I discovered that what I was witnessing was a pattern of behaviour that had been repeated time and time again. I had been so involved with myself up until now that I hadn't noticed what had been going on right under my nose all this time. I resolved to investigate further.

Next meal time, it was Hairy that was doing the honours. I was, I must admit, a little reticent about eating. Given my state of mind, that's hardly surprising. And then Hairy did something that he'd often done in the past. He got a spoonful of the food and made a big fuss of eating it himself and, in a very exaggerated manner, expressed just how yummy it was by going 'Mmmmmmmmmm!!!!' I had always assumed that this course of action was an encouragement to get me to eat. ( Like that's going to work.) Now I realised that what was actually going on was something much simpler. And much sadder.

Hairy was using the cover of pretending to encourage me to get to eat as a way of getting some obviously much needed nutrition for himself. And the very theatrical,  OTT reaction of 'Mmmmmmmm!!!!' was neither theatrical nor OTT. It was just honest. Given just how unappetising the food was, such a reaction just goes to show just how poverty-stricken Hairy must be.  I couldn't eat a thing. I had completely lost my appetite. Each time Hairy brought the spoon to my mouth I spun my head away. This was precisely the right thing to do. When Hairy released me from the high chair, my bowl was still full of food. I decided to busy myself on the floor and just keep an eye on the proceedings. Hairy, seeing I was occupied on the floor, ate up everything that was in the bowl. My refusing to eat had meant that Hairy at last got a decent meal. I saw it not so much as an act of charity, but as an act of simple humanity.

Next meal time I was back with Smooth. I decided to try out a ruse. I threw a bit of fish finger on the floor. Smooth picked it up and ate it. I almost wept. Can there be any indignity so great as being reduced to scavenging for scraps flung from the tables of those that have? I was ashamed at having tried so degrading an experiment. I felt, somehow, grubby. (Admittedly I am often actually grubby, but this was an altogether different, inner, grubbiness.) But gaining a little insight and humility can't, in the long run, be a bad thing. Especially if you figure out a way of doing something about the situation you encountered. And I did.

What I resolved to do is always leave some food in the bowl. And always to throw a fair amount of food on the floor. That way I can be sure that Hairy and Smooth get something to eat every day. It's not about charity, it's about humanity. After all, how can I eat when those about me can't?

# 'Charlie Don't Surf.' A Few Final Thoughts On The Baby Monitor Wars

Looking back on the whole episode I think I've learned several valuable lessons. First, never be afraid of the size of your opponent.

Second, if you're small, fast and manoeuvrable enough you've always got a chance of blowing up The Death Star.

Third, and I recourse here to a quote from Lev Davidovich Bronstein Trotsky, 'Where force is necessary, one should make use of it boldly, resolutely, and right to the end. But it is as well to know the limitations of force; to know where to combine force with manoeuvre, assault with conciliation.'

Finally, and perhaps this is the most important lesson of all, before you prepare to sacrifice everything for the good of the cause, make sure the cause is worth the sacrifice.

# MONTH XXI

Humpty Dumpty. Did he fall or was he pushed?
If only it were that simple.

# Send Three And Fourpence
# We're Going To A Dance

In my opinion what I say is perfectly comprehensible. I utter words, I construct sentences, I build whole, coherent, compelling arguments. Unfortunately, both Hairy and Smooth are so intellectually challenged that they understand not one single syllable. I engage them in conversation, they seem to be taking in what I'm saying, but as soon as they open their mouths to reply it's patently obvious that they haven't understood a single thing I've said. I'm trapped in a nightmare world peopled with physical giants but mental pygmies. As far as they're concerned, I might as well be speaking scribble.

But then, the other day, I thought we'd made a breakthrough. I was sitting on the floor toying with, and considering, one of the shoes I had filed away the night before under my cot in between a half-chewed rusk and my least favourite dummy. I looked up to find Smooth in attendance perusing my every move. I went back to what I was doing. When I looked up again she was still there, watching. I became a little embarrassed with the whole situation. To ease the tension I decided to try and include Smooth in what I was doing and engaged her in conversation about this shoe. My precise words escape me, but I think that the gist of my thesis was that, although the shoe was a functional piece, it hardly paid any heed to the pioneering fashion work of the likes of Patrick Cox, Manolo

Blahnik or the grittier urban street chic of Dr Marten.

Smooth followed every word I said. Or so it seemed. She opened her mouth to speak. For one brief, glorious, instant I thought we were on the verge of a breakthrough. It was going to be like that climactic moment in *Close Encounters of the Third Kind* when the mothership booms back that simple, haunting phrase - doo doo doo doo doooo. (Obviously this last sentence works much better if you know the tune.)

I waited with bated breath. Smooth's lips parted.

'Shoe' she said. A good, if somewhat self evident, start. I sat, stared and concentrated, eager not to miss a single nuance of how the sentence would develop. 'Shoe' said Smooth again. Then she pointed to the shoe and for the third time uttered one single word. 'Shoe'.

I was living with an imbecile. I know that the art of conversation is supposed to be dead, but this was ridiculous. And it got worse. Smooth picked up the shoe, held it up to my face, and in a slow, stupid, but perfectly enunciated voice said 'Shooooooooooe'.

I ran screaming from the room.

There was no avoiding it, if I was going to get anywhere with Hairy and Smooth I was going to have to learn to speak a language they understood. Not yet two and already I was going to have to be bi-lingual.

# I Am A Fugitive From A Reins Gang

**R**eins, on my high chair at meal-times, I can handle. I'm not saying that I like the things, but I accept them. They've always been there. In short, reins on my high chair, I don't have a problem with.

Apparently, that's not enough for some people. Apparently, some people think reins should be introduced in other arenas of my life. All I can say is 'I think not'.

It all started as we were preparing to go out one day. I'd been ready ages, but Smooth was spending absolute aeons faffing about. I busied myself in the hall chewing the letters that lay on the mat. At last, Smooth headed my way, closely followed by Hairy.

I should have realised that something was afoot. They don't usually act in concert. Not unless they're up to something. All I can say in my defence is that I was distracted by a particularly tasty envelope. The next thing I knew, the reins were half on. I was too shocked to comprehend the full magnitude of events.

Before I knew it, the reins were fully on and we were out the door. I walked, tentatively, down the front path. Smooth followed a few steps behind. Hairy walked by her side. I reached the pavement and turned to look at my entourage. They looked at me, smiling. I looked at them, looked at

the reins strapped to my torso, then back at them. They continued to smile. In retrospect there was altogether too much smiling, but at the time I was lulled into a false sense of security. Apart from the fact that there was an extra something attached to my body, everything seemed to be normal. So I, fool that I am, carried on as normal.

We walked on down the street as we had many a time before. Then, like many a time before, I spotted a crisp packet blowing along the pavement. I executed a pretty smart 180 degree turn and set off in hot pursuit. Barely half-way to my intended prey, an invisible hand was thrust into my chest and stopped me in my tracks. I tried again to reach my booty which was now just that little bit further away. Same result.

I turned toward Smooth and Hairy to see if any explanation for my predicament was forthcoming. All I got was another smile. Slightly forced, but a smile nonetheless. I attempted once more to pursue the crisp packet, by now almost out of sight. Once more the invisible hand on my chest curtailed my endeavour. I looked down at my chest and my gaze came to rest on that alien attachment – the reins. All became clear.

The rest of that trip was a nightmare. I couldn't go anywhere I wanted. I was restrained by those dreadful reins, attached to my own particular ball and chain – Smooth. What on earth is going on? They spend an eternity trying to get me to walk, then, when I can, all they want to do is stop me. Is there any logic in this universe?

# Perchance To Nap

I think it was Cervantes in Don Quixote who said:

*God bless whoever invented sleep, the dark cloak that covers all human thoughts. It is the food that satisfies hunger, the water that quenches thirst, the fire that warms cold, the cold that reduces heat, and, lastly, the common currency which can buy anything, the balance and compensating weight that makes the shepherd equal to the king, and the simpleton equal to the sage.*

In many ways I agree. Sleep is brilliant. However, I would qualify my appreciation of the virtues of sleep by saying that you have to be in the right mood. When sleep is forced upon you when you're not ready for it, it is quite a different beaker of juice. In these cases you could say, in my view, (with apologies to the maestro Miguel de'):

*God curse whoever invented sleep, the sleepy suit that stifles all human thought. It is the cold porridge that is very yuk, the sour milk that makes thirst retch, it is the shelf just out of reach, the drawer that traps your fingers and will not open, and, lastly the senseless blankness that makes Teddy Bear equal to Piggy, and turns today into tomorrow.*

Now, turning today into tomorrow may not be a bad thing,

 but if you're having a really good time today, why would you want tomorrow to turn up?

Which brings me to the matter of napping. A nap is a sleep of a strictly limited duration. A nap can only happen during the day. And for some reason, a nap will inevitably at some stage in your relationship with Hairy and Smooth become 'an issue'.

The point of a nap is that it gives you a chance to get away from Hairy and Smooth when they start to get tired and fractious. It gives you the chance to collect your thoughts while they calm down. Many a time when I've been up ages reorganising things (why do they always put things in the wrong cupboards and the wrong drawers?) I look across at H or S and notice that they're getting very flustered. So I go for a nap. And when I wake up again, the transformation in their whole attitude, demeanour and mood is remarkable.

The other day things worked out decidedly differently. And it was all because I didn't fancy a nap. On the face of it, that doesn't sound such a major trauma. You should have seen the state that Smooth got into. Three times she put me in my cot and tried to get me to lie down. Well, I was having none of it. The first time she put me in I calmly explained to her that, grateful though I was for being afforded this opportunity to nap, I actually had been rather busy. The second time I expressed myself a little more forcefully. The third time, frustrated by the cavalier way in which my wishes were being treated, I threw everything out of the cot and onto the floor.

Smooth finally got the message. She released me from my bondage. And, in a move that I see very much as a gesture of apology on her part, she took me to the park in the buggy. All I can say about the subsequent sequence of events is that all that cot protest work must have tired me out. That's why as soon as Smooth lifted me into a swing I drifted off to sleep. I remember her face, in close-up, staring at me, frowning. I just don't get it; you'd think she'd be happy.

Then there are the days that you don't nap at all. Boy do they hate that.

But there is one thing worse. I speak, of course, of the Late Afternoon Nap. The Late Afternoon Nap means that when you do finally get up you have loads of energy so you can stay up for ages doing things.

Now why should that be such a big problem?

# How I Spent The Whole Of One Day And Half Of One Night This Month For No Reason In Particular That I Can Figure Out

Waaaaaaaaaaaaaaaaaaaaaaaaaaaaaaaaaaaaaaaaaaaaaaaaaaaaaaa
aaaaaaaaaaaaaaaaaaaaaaaaaaaaaaaaaaaaaaaaaaaaaaaaaaaaaaaaa
aaaaaaaaaaaaaaaaaaaaaaaaaaaaaaaaaaaaaaaaaaaaaaaaaaaaaaaaa
aaaaaaaaaaaaaaaaaaaaaaaaaaaaaaaaaaaaaaaaaaaaaaaaaaaaaaaaa
aaaaaaaaaaaaaaaaaaaaaaaaaaaaaaaaaaaaaaaaaaaaaaaaaaaaaaaaa
aaaaaaaaaaaaaaaaaaaaaaaaaaaaaaaaaaaaaaaaaaaaaaaaaaaaaaaaa
aaaaaaaaaaaaaaaaaaaaaaaaaaaaaaaaaaaaaaaaaaaaaaaaaaaaaaaaa
aaaaaaaaaaaaaaaaaaaaaaaaaaaaaaaaaaaaaaaaaaaaaaaaaaaaaaaaa
aaaaaaaaaaaaaaaaaaaaaaaaaaaaaaaaaaaaaaaaaaaaaaaaaaaaaaaaa
aaaaaaaaaaaaaaaaaaaaaaaaaaaaaaaaaaaaaaaaaaaaaaaaaaaaaaaaa
aaaaaaaaaaaaaaaaaaaaaaaaaaaaaaaaaaaaaaaaaaaaaaaaaaaaaaaaa
aaaaaaaaaaaaaaaaaaaaaaaaaaaaaaaaaaaaaaaaaaaaaaaaaaaaaaaaa
aaaaaaaaaaaaaaaaaaaaaaaaaaaaaaaaaaaaaaaaaaaaaaaaaaaaaaaaa
aaaaaaaaaaaaaaaaaaaaaaaaaaaaaaaaaaaaaaaaaaaaaaaaaaaaaaaaa
aaaaaaaaaaaaaaaaaaaaaaaaaaaaaaaaaaaaaaaaaaaaaaaaaaaaaaaaa
aaaaaaaaaaaaaaaaaaaaaaaaaaaaaaaaaaaaaaaaaaaaaaaaaaaaaaaaa
aaaaaaaaaaaaaaaaaaaaaaaaaaaaaaaaaaaaaaaaaaaaaaaaaaaaaaaaa
aaaaaaaaaaaaaaaaaaaaaaaaaaaaaaaaaaaaaaaaaaaaaaaaaaaaaaaaa
aaaaaaaaaaaaaaaaaaaaaaaaaaaaaaaaaaaaaaaaaaaaaaaaaaaaaaaaa
aaaaaaaaaaaaaaaaaaaaaaaaaaaaaaaaaaaaaaaaaaaaaaaaaaaaaaaaa
aaaaaaaaaaaaaaaaaaaaaaaaaaaaaaaaaaaaaaaaaaaaaaaaaaaaaaaaa
aaaaaaaaaaaaaaaaaaaaaaaaaaaaaaaaaaaaaaaaaaaaaaaaaaaaaaaaa
aaaaaaaaaaaaaaaaaaaaaaaaaaaaaaaaaaaaaaaaaaaaaaaaaaaaaaaaa

aaaaaaaaaaaaaaaaaaaaaaaaaaaaaaaaaaaaaaaaaaaaaaaaaaaaaaaa
aaaaaaaaaaaaaaaaaaaaaaaaaaaaaaaaaaaaaaaaaaaaaaaaaaaaaaaa
aaaaaaaaaaaaaaaaaaaaaaaaaaaaaaaaaaaaaaaaaaaaaaaaaaaaaaaa
aaaaaaaaaaaaaaaaaaaaaaaaaaaaaaaaaaaaaaaaaaaaaaaaaaaaaaaa
aaaaaaaaaaaaaaaaaaaaaaaaaaaaaaaaaaaaaaaaaaaaaaaaaaaaaaaa
aaaaaaaaaaaaaaaaaaaaaaaaaaaaaaaaaaaaaaaaaaaaaaaaaaaaaaaa
aaaaaaaaaaaaaaaaaaaaaaaaaaaaaaaaaaaaaaaaaaaaaaaaaaaaaaaa
aaaaaaaaaaaaaaaaaaaaaaaaaaaaaaaaaaaaaaaaaaaaaaaaaaaaaaaa
aaaaaaaaaaaaaaaaaaaaaaaaaaaaaaaaaaaaaaaaaaaaaaaaaaaaaaaa
aaaaaaaaaaaaaaaaaaaaaaaaaaaaaaaaaaaaaaaaaaaaaaaaaaaaaaaa
aaaaaaaaaaaaaaaaaaaaaaaaaaaaaaaaaaaaaaaaaaaaaaaaaaaaaaaa
aaaaaaaaaaaaaaaaaaaaaaaaaaaaaaaaaaaaaaaaaaaaaaaaaaaaaaaa
aaaaaaaaaaaaaaaaaaaaaaaaaaaaaaaaaaaaaaaaaaaaaaaaaaaaaaaa
aaaaaaaaaaaaaaaaaaaaaaaaaaaaaaaaaaaaaaaaaaaaaaaaaaaaaaaa
aaaaaaaaaaaaaaaaaaaaaaaaaaaaaaaaaaaaaaaaaaaaaaaaaaaaaaaa
aaaaaaaaaaaaaaaaaaaaaaaaaaaaaaaaaaaaaaaaaaaaaaaaaaaaaaaa
aaaaaaaaaaaaaaaaaaaaaaaaaaaaaaaaaaaaaaaaaaaaaaaaaaaaaaaa
aaaaaaaaaaaaaaaaaaaaaaaaaaaaaaaaaaaaaaaaaaaaaaaaaaaaaaaa
aaaaaaaaaaaaaaaaaaaaaaaaaaaaaaaaaaaaaaaaaaaaaaaaaaaaaaaa
aaaaaaaaaaaaaaaaaaaaaaaaaaaaaaaaaaaaaaaaaaaaaaaaaaaaaaaa
aaaaaaaaaaaaaaaaaaaaaaaaaaaaaaaaaaaaaaaaaaaaaaaaaaaaaaaa
aaaaaaaaaaaaaaaaaaaaaaaaaaaaaaaaaaaaaaaaaaaaaaaaaaaaaaaa
aaaaaaaaaaaaaaaaaaaaaaaaaaaaaaaaaaaaaaaaaaaaaaaaaaaaaaaa
aaaaaaaaaaaaaaaaaaaaaaaaaaaaaaaaaaaaaaaaaaaaaaaaaaaaaaaa
aaaaaaaaaaaaaaaaaaaaaaaaaaaaaaaaaaaaaaaaaaaaaaaaaaaaaaaa
aaaaaaaaaaaaaaaaaaaaaaaaaaaaaaaaaaaaaaaaaaaaaaaaaaaaaaaa
aaaaaaaaaaaaaaaaaaaaaaaaaaaaaaaaaaaaaaaaaaaaaaaaaaaaaaaa
aaaaaaaaaaaaaaaaaaaaaaaaaaaaaaaaaaaaaaaaaaaaaaaaaaaaaaaa
aaaaaaaaaaaaaaaaaaaaaaaaaaaaaaaaaaaaaaaaaaaaaaaaaaaaaaaa
aaaaaaaaaaaaaaaaaaaaaaaaaaaaaaaaaaaaaaaaaaaaaaaaaaaaaaaa

**aaaaaaaaaah!**

# Yes I Know It's Just A Manky Old Piece Of Blanket But It Makes Me Happy

**U**ntil now I've been kind of embarrassed to talk about this. That's why although it's been with me quite a lot of the time, I haven't ever mentioned it before. Now that I'm just that little bit more mature, I've realised that it's a very foolish individual who thinks they can get through life without a little support. So why not talk about it?

I call it My Comfy. It doesn't look like much, but it's kind of special. We've been through so much together. Whenever I've needed friendship and support, My Comfy's been there for me. Its touch is warm and soft and familiar. Its smell is the smell of comfort. And its taste is so incredibly blankety that it's like the distilled essence of a thousand blankets that have lived full, meaningful, beautiful lives.

My Comfy has been in or around my life for as long as I can remember. However, it is only in this second year that I have really come to appreciate its true qualities. I put this down to the fact it is only now that I am really beginning to understand just how complex and complicated the world is. Faced with such confusion, is it not totally understandable that I should like to have something familiar with me wherever I go? Viewed objectively, My Comfy actually doesn't do much to help me in any given set of circumstances, but to be honest, that's not really the point of it. Sometimes just being there helps.

My Comfy proved a true friend the first time I encountered The Long Nosed Sucky Beast (LNSB). I was happily investigating whether carpets in different rooms tasted the same, when an appalling racket started. The most hellish apparition manifested itself, dragging Smooth behind it. As I watched, horrified, it made its way towards me. Then, in its path, I spotted half a breadstick I had squashed into the carpet that morning in order to have a snack later in the day. Under my very nose, the LNSB pounced upon it and gulped it down. Not only did the creature eat the breadstick — my breadstick — but you could see it being digested in the monster's swirling, shrieking guts. Nightmare!

I backed away from the LNSB and grabbed My Comfy from where I'd hidden it under the sofa. The second I felt the soft warmth of its touch, reassurance flooded my shaking frame. Emboldened, I approached the monster. It was then that I felt My Comfy being snatched away.

I couldn't believe what was happening. The LNSB was trying to eat My Comfy. I tightened my grip on my compatriot and screamed in rage at the monster and its monstrous plan. I needn't have worried. My Comfy, despite its soft, warm and cuddly exterior, obviously has a steely interior and the heart of a warrior. The Beast had devoured barely a fraction of my pal when the noise it was making changed. From the roar of the marauding conqueror to the whine of a defeated, dejected enemy. And then it stopped dead in its tracks. In silence.

Smooth extricated My Comfy from the jaws of the vanquished foe, and dragged its carcass away. I hugged that tattered piece of blanket to me in an astonished embrace. At that moment, I truly knew that whatever perils I faced in the world, if My Comfy were by my side I would never, ever be alone.

My Comfy? My Hero.

# Nursery Crimes Five.
# How Long Can It Be Before Oliver Stone
# Makes The Movie?

'Humpty Dumpty sat on a wall.
Humpty Dumpty had a great fall.
All the King's horses, and all the King's men
Couldn't put Humpty together again.'

Nightmare, nightmare, nightmare. A rhyme with many
sinister and unresolved layers of meaning.

The guy is essentially a giant egg with little arms and legs.
He is a freakish cross between man and egg. He is, in a very
real sense, The Eggman. And not a 'coo-coo ca-choo' in sight.

Where Mr H. D. hails from is never revealed. No personal
history, no parental information, no context is ever
forthcoming. Indeed how on earth do you end up with an
individual who's half-man and half-egg? No light is shed on
any of these matters no matter how assiduously one
analyses the text.

Which brings me to the predicament young Humpty finds
himself, i.e. sitting on a wall. Doesn't that sound just a little
bit fishy? How does a large egg with fairly stubby arms and
legs actually find himself on a wall?

Some pictures I've seen indicate the use of a ladder, but
who put it there? And why? Maybe, just maybe, the ladder is
a red herring. Or maybe, the ladder is the vital clue that

reveals that what we're dealing with here isn't a simple, but tragic accident, but that we are now in fact through the looking glass and find ourselves mired in a most appalling conspiracy and the possibility of foul play.

So why is he up there? And how did he get there?

Even more: what on earth were the King's horses and King's men doing there? Coincidence? I think not. And how do we know that they really tried to 'put Humpty together again'? Cast yourself if you will in the position of one of the King's men. You arrive at the scene of the 'accident'. You leap from your trusty steed and your humanitarian instincts spring into action and your first thought is 'I must try and put him together again'. But that doesn't match the text.

Rewinding this little scenario in which you're one of the King's men, you arrive at the wall, you survey the carnage, you decide to try and 'put Humpty together again', and then you let your horse help. Now unless 'the King's horses' have been spending their quiet moments in the stables doing jigsaw puzzles, getting them to help in the intricate and delicate task of reassembling the boy Humpty is hardly the act of a budding Florence Nightingale.

If the King's men are involved, what about the King? It is an extremely loaded question and the implications for the monarchy as a whole are immense.

So what's my explanation for what went on?

I have none. Because, frankly, there isn't enough evidence one way or the other. There is nothing in the tale as told that would stand up to scrutiny in a court of law. All I can offer is conjecture. I leave it up to you to decide if there's anything in the possibilities I put forward. So here goes.

A What if Humpty Dumpty were the illegitimate son of the King and some lowly egg who took his fancy in the Palace larder late one night after a particularly lavish banquet?

B What if, as the child grew up, the King allowed him to stay in the palace as playmate for his own legitimate offspring?

C What if, when his own kids left home, the King found the continued presence of Humpty an embarrassment, an embarrassment who held within his brittle shell the possibility of scandal, should the truth ever come out?

D What if, in a moment of frustration, the King one day cried out 'Who will rid me of this troublesome Humpty?'

E And what if one of the King's men heard the outburst?

Now Humpty might have always been on very good terms with the King's men, so that when they came to him and suggested they had a new game to play, who's to say he didn't leap at the chance?

Maybe they reassured him as they carried him laughing up the ladder. Maybe they joked as they went down again, leaving him sitting on the wall. And maybe they then went and hid behind the wall, in silence, and waited for the inevitable to happen.

So maybe it was an accident that ended Humpty's days as he tried, under his own steam, with his own stubby arms and legs, to get down from the wall and back to the Palace.

Or maybe, just maybe, as Humpty sat on the wall, surveyed his surroundings, and pondered his lot, the façade of privilege that was his life at the Palace finally cracked. Maybe he realised that there's little hope for happiness for a half-man, half-egg in a world where all too often, to be different, is to be despised. So maybe he jumped. All I'll add is, should a mysterious accident happen to me, check the floor round my cot for hoof marks.

# An Apology

I've just re-read the piece on Humpty Dumpty. I think I
got a bit carried away. Sorry.
I really must stop eating cheese just before I go to bed.

# Lost

We were in the supermarket. We being Smooth and myself. Ordinarily when we visit the supermarket I get to travel in a most odd contraption. It's kind of a cross between a buggy and a cot. And it has very thin, very cold, bars. I sit high up on the side of it looking toward Smooth as she pushes it around. I have no complaints with the cruising altitude as it affords me a very commanding view. But the direction of travel is an altogether different matter. My position means that I'm sitting with my back towards the direction we're going in. I hate that. Also it means that when Smooth picks up stuff and deposits it in the buggy/cot (or should that be cot/buggy?) I can't see what the stuff is. Now how annoying is that?

But this visit was different. This visit Smooth carried me. The advantage of being carried is that you're even higher so you see even more, and different, things. The disadvantages are that your personal space is totally compromised and your opportunities for action are decidedly curtailed.

For some reason, trips that involve carrying don't last very long, so it's important to feast on as much visual stimulation as possible because you'll soon be out of there. Which is how come I spotted a big pile of tins that looked very much, in construction, like the big pile of building blocks that Hairy sometimes builds for me to knock over. Anyway I was just musing on whether the tins would be as aesthetically pleasing as bricks if they were knocked over, when the oddest thing happened. Smooth put me down. Then she turned away from me and stretched up with both hands to get something off a high shelf.

Opportunity is a rusk you only get one chance to suck, as we say amongst my people. So I nipped back to where I'd seen the tower of tins to resolve my aesthetic theory. I suppose I must have taken the wrong turning, because when I got to where I was going I discovered it wasn't where I was going at all. The tower of tins was nowhere to be seen. I searched high and low — well as high as I could search given that as yet I'm not really of a stature to be asked to stand at the back in group photos. But no joy. So I went back to Smooth. But Smooth wasn't where I had left her. Horror of horrors, she must have wandered off.

What was I going to do? The first thing I thought was 'don't panic. Just look for her. She can't have gone far.' I was just about to do that when another thought occurred to me. In retrospect, it's not a thought that I'm particularly proud of, but I did think it. So I'll share it with you and trust that you won't judge me too harshly for it. I thought, 'I'm free. I've got no responsibilities. I can please myself. I can go where I want. Do what I want. Be who I want. I'm beholden to no one.'

But then reality kicked in. Smooth was all alone. Anything could happen to her. I had to find her. How on earth would I be able to explain things to Hairy if anything did happen. Especially as I couldn't speak.

I started to search. First I moved with slow deliberation scanning the knees of everyone I encountered for that familiar chubbily quality that would signal I had discovered

Smooth. As I moved from aisle to aisle amid a forest of alien knees, I felt fear welling up inside me. I started to move faster. I ran from place to place. Smooth was out there all alone. Anything could be happening to her. Tears filled my eyes. Not only could I not see Smooth, but I couldn't see anything. Fear gave way to panic. I ran blindly from one place to another. I didn't mean to find the tower of tins. I mean, if I'd meant to find the tower of tins I think I probably would have stopped before running straight into them. But I didn't. They crashed all around me in a hail of explosions. I have no idea how aesthetically pleasing the sight and sound was. I was too busy plummeting from panic into hysteria. I had to find Smooth. She was all alone.

I let out a wail of sheer frustration at the futility of my plight. And that, I think, is what finally worked. Smooth must have heard the cry. And she found me. All I can say is that she must have been really scared at being all alone because she was in tears when she appeared.

We went home. I comforted her as best I could. It had been a very close shave.

# Then One Day The Teacher Leaves The Room And, Out Of The Blue, Puts You In Charge

The night after the incident in the supermarket I couldn't get to sleep. I tossed and turned and turned and tossed. I moved my compatriots from one end of the cot to the other, then back again. I pulled up the sheet and draped it over my shoulders. Then I draped it over my head. Then I draped it over the side of the cot where it fell to the floor. (That brought an end to the draping.) I lay on my back. I lay on my front. I even got into a crouch and walked round the cot like Groucho Marx. Nothing helped. I just couldn't clear my mind of what had happened.

But what really disturbed me was that I couldn't clear my head of what might have happened. Smooth had been all alone. Anything could have happened. Anything.

1 She could have fallen over.
2 She could have fallen over and hit her head really hard and started to cry and then run round looking for someone to comfort her but then run into the corner of a table and poked herself in that bit just above her eye so that it hurt even more and she had to cry even harder. (Believe me, it happens.)
3 She could have filled her nappy and have no one to change it.
4 She could have been pushed over by someone bigger.

5 She could have caught her fingers in a door.

6 She could have crawled into a small space and not been able to get out.

7 She could have picked up something from the floor and tried eating it only to discover that it was incredibly yuk.

8 She could have been abducted by aliens made of porridge. (I don't know where this came from. In retrospect, it's unlikely. I don't think I even know what an alien is apart from that brief glimpse on *The X Files*.)

9 All her hair could have got caught up in a giant piece of velcro and had to be extricated by someone in a real hurry.

10 Well, I'll leave 10 blank so that you can fill in your own personal nightmare.

Is it any wonder that I didn't get any sleep. Through history there have been many great moments of revelation. St Paul on the road to Damascus. Archimedes leaping out of the bath, shouting 'Eureka!' That bit at the end of *The Usual Suspects* when the detective finally realises Kevin Spacey has been lying all along.

And there was this.

'I am totally responsible for Smooth.'

It doesn't sound like much, but think about it. Her well-being, her development, her happiness, her safety, are all down to me. Even writing it down now, when I've had plenty of time to get used to the idea, makes me pause for thought. In fact, I think I need to go and lie down.

# MONTH XXII

Richard Milhous Nixon, when he was trying to squirm his
way out of the Watergate débâcle, said something along the
lines of, 'I was responsible, but I was not to blame'. Sorry
Dickie, nice try but no cigar. Responsibility just doesn't
work that way.

# In Which I'm Just About Getting To Grips With The Hard Facts Of Reality When Along Comes Something That Rewrites The Rules

In the comparatively short time that I have been wandering about checking out the gloriously muddled fray that is life, I have spotted there is one thing, above all else, that society craves. Structure.

Order confers upon society a degree of coherence. Order also provides a set of rules and boundaries within which the individual can operate and, perhaps more importantly, against which the individual can rebel. And the urge to rebel, to bend the rules, to break the rules, to feign complete ignorance of the existence of the rules, is all part of the process of developing. Hence, when I casually wander over to the video recorder and try to see if, by inserting a jam sandwich into it and pushing the relevant buttons, it's possible to watch that particular jam sandwich on the television, this is not an aimless act. No matter how great my air of insouciance, I know I am doing 'wrong' and I know my actions will undoubtedly end in a swift rebuke. But that is why I am doing it. Physically I may be pushing in a jam sandwich, but metaphorically I am pushing at a set of boundaries. (I must admit that on one memorable occasion I did actually get the jam sandwich into the video and because neither Hairy or Smooth were in the room, the lack of the expected admonition threw me off balance, so I ran out of the room and went and hid under my cot.) What I'm saying is that society craves the existence of order and rules not only as a way of structuring itself, but also as strops against which the razor of individuality can be honed.

Occasionally, however, something comes along that tips all the toys out of the buggy.

Salvador Dali's melting watch, for instance. Or René Magritte's bloke with a bowler hat on and an apple in front of his face. Or Marcel Duchamp's seminal urinal. Or, more recently, Damien Hirst's shark in aspic. To your run-of-the-mill punter who may not know about art, but knows what they like, the first encounter with any of these works must have been a quite considerable shock.

Which is pretty much how I felt the first time I happened upon the bizarre phenomenon that is The Bouncy Castle.

What on earth is The Bouncy Castle all about? Its properties are easy to describe. It is a castle. It is bouncy. It's not that I've got anything against bounciness per se, it's just that it's a quality that I find somewhat disquieting in a building. Bounciness, in its place, is a fantastic thing. A bed is a gloriously bouncy affair. So is a sofa. So is Hairy's tummy (though he seems not to think so). Many a productive and enjoyable hour can be spent bouncing around on any of them.

Tigger, too, is notoriously bouncy. Many people put down his bounciness to the fact that, according to the song, 'his body is made out of rubber and his tail is made out of spring'. I'm of the school of thought that attributes Tigger's bounciness to an inner, fundamental bounciness of the soul. Bouncing in Tigger is a totally understandable and admirable thing. Bouncing in a building is a completely different size of nappy. It is unnatural. It is illogical. And it is absurd.

But I love it.

From the very instant I first set foot on my first Bouncy Castle, I was lost. Maybe it was the total ludicrousness of it all that won me over. Maybe it was the looks of utter joy on the faces of my co-bouncees. Or maybe it was just the sheer, unadulterated, unapologetic bounciness of it all. From my very first bounce I was a convert. And as I fly, unfettered, skywards, only one query troubles my sensation-flooded consciousness.

Why just Bouncy Castles? Why not Bouncy Houses? Or Bouncy Offices? Or Bouncy Dry Cleaners?

# A Brief Mention Of One Of The Most Satisfying Feelings In The World

There's nothing quite like doing a poo in a nappy that's just been put on.

# Absurdity, Rhythm And The Gaps Between Words. Or Beckett, Mamet, Pinter And Me

I've been thinking about language development. Conventional wisdom has it that as I learn to speak words Hairy and Smooth can understand, I am at last mastering language and actually learning to express myself. Conventional wisdom has it that up until now I have done little more than speak scribble.

I put it to you that conventional wisdom is wrong.

My point is that I am not, at last, learning language, but am actually learning another language. It is cultural arrogance of the highest order to assume just because Hairy and Smooth can't understand my language, then obviously I don't have one. I do. It is a complex and vibrant language and it also works.

Admittedly, Hairy and Smooth may not be party to its full beauty or subtlety, but on the whole they get what I'm going on about. They know when I'm hungry, they know when I'm happy, they know when I'm sad, they know when I'm tired, they know when I need changing. I have a language perfectly suited for my needs. The necessity for me to learn a second language only arises because my needs are changing. But before I leave my language behind, I want to explore it in more depth, and make some important connections.

There is an inherent absurdity in the language I speak. That's because the world I operate in is absurd. Frankly, so much doesn't make sense, it's remarkable that anything I get to talk about is coherent. For instance, why is it that Hairy and Smooth spent ages encouraging me to walk, then when I master that particular skill they spend most of their time stopping me from running around?

Which brings me to one of the great masters of communication, S. Beckett. He too seems to inhabit a nonsensical, surreal world that he describes via nonsensical, surreal language. Take his masterpiece *Waiting For Godot*. If that's not about two people trapped in a cot of a morning and trying to make sense of what happened yesterday and of what might happen today, then I'll eat my nappy. Indeed, the seemingly aimless meandering of the dialogue could have been lifted verbatim from many of the early morning conversations I have had in my cot with Teddy Bear. (Not that Teddy Bear says much.) As for who, precisely, is 'Godot'; well if you're detained by that question then I believe you're missing the point. The thing is that 'Godot' doesn't come. Which is why, to my mind 'Godot', whose arrival seems to promise order, structure and meaning for Vladimir and Estragon, is in fact a euphemism for 'tomorrow'. But, I'm getting off the point. All I'm trying to say is that, as in the Beckettian universe, there is a great deal of nonsense and surrealism in my language. I mean, you have to admit that it is rather amusing that one of the first words I used to bridge the gulf between me and Hairy and Smooth was 'Dada'.

Which brings me to Mamet. Mamet's language relates to mine in its musicality. There is a rhythm, a pitch and a tone in his language. Likewise in mine. However, I like to think that my language has more variation than his. Classic Mamet seems to be all about staccato rhythms and fractured dialogue. Occasionally he employs a longer, rambling monologue. I regularly use all his techniques but I hold a full house to his two pair as I also have at my disposal the glory that is the sustained wail. As far as I am aware in none of Mamet's plays do any of his characters let out a long, full-blooded wail. Big mistake, Davey boy.

The wail is a glorious piece of primordial, almost non-verbal communication. I can only put Mamet's reluctance to employ it down to a lack of bottle. The wail can be so expressive. There's the Rising Wail, the Falling Wail, the Rising and Falling Wail, the Interrupted Wail, the Wail-and-Sob, the Wail-and-Shriek, the Wail-Sob-Shriek-and-Holler, the Demi-Wail, the Muffled Wail, the Moroccan Wail and the Pseudo-Wail, to name but a few. Where Mamet scores over me is that his characters speak actual words. But, take it from me, as a means of communication words are a pretty flawed medium. They obscure as much as they reveal.

Finally there's Harold P, the universally acknowledged master of the pause. Dialogue that includes numerous pauses is often called 'Pinteresque'. If so, then almost everything I say is 'Pinteresque'. In fact, you could say that it is beyond 'Pinteresque' because I am a devotee of pauses broken up by the occasional bit of

dialogue. The other day, for instance, Smooth picked me up and asked me if I wanted my nappy changed. I looked at her, said nothing for an age, then replied (not that she could understand) that Po was my favourite Tellytubby. Pure Pinter. Absolutely pure Pinter. As a piece of dialogue you could drop it into *The Birthday Party* and no one would notice the difference. Apart from Harold P, of course. He would go ballistic. And rightly so.

I suppose, in summation, I feel such a great affinity for the works of these three dramatists because their language, like mine, comprises of absurdities, rhythms, and meanings communicated in the gaps between words. Their language, and how they use it, is precise. And pure. As is mine. If only anyone could understand.

That's why, as I embark on learning the language of Hairy and Smooth, I leave behind my own particular Tower of Babble with no little sadness. I'll miss its precision. And its expressiveness.

But I'm not dumping it all. No matter how adept I get at manipulating my new vocabulary I'll always keep a place of honour for the good old wail.

# Remote Control. Or How To Manipulate, Intimidate And Demoralise The Opposition Without Doing A Single Thing

What you do is go into a different room, or to a place where you can't be seen, and just wait very quietly. That's all you do, absolutely nothing. It won't take long before Hairy or Smooth has to stop whatever they're doing and come in and see you. And that's when you give them the knowing look.* Trust me, they'll know that they've lost.

*For this technique it's best to practise a look that says 'you poor sap. I've done absolutely nothing and yet I've bent you to my will. Just think how powerless to resist you're going to be when I decide to actually do things to control you. And by the way you've got a porridge stain all down your leg. Hah!'

# Hugs, Kisses And Cuddles

**H**ugging, kissing and cuddling should be avoided at all times. Basically, you're fraternising with the enemy. Unfortunately, H, K and C are wonderful.

Indeed, they are so wonderful that I indulge in them fairly frequently. In fact, I would say hardly a day goes by without me getting into a fairly involved bout of H, K and C. All of which has led me to question the received wisdom amongst my people that it is something we shouldn't do. How can something that feels so good be wrong?

However, wander down that particular path of thought and you soon find yourself staring at the very foundations of everything you believe in. What I'm getting at is the deeply unsettling idea that maybe the parents aren't the enemy.

It's a thought I refuse to contemplate. The implications are far too great. Look at it in the context of history (one of the top contexts to look at things in) and it would be like discovering that the earth goes round the sun, that we are the product of evolution, and that Milli Vanilli were miming, all on the same morning.

And yet I can't deny the evidence of my senses. Hugging, kissing and cuddling make me feel good. They make me feel warm. They make me feel safe. They make me feel wanted. They make me feel relaxed. They make me feel excited. They make me feel all these things, all at the same time.

There must be a better way of expressing all this, but I don't know what it is.

# Before You Think I'm Losing My Edge

In case that last piece makes you think I'm going soft, let me swiftly disabuse you of your misapprehension. I'm not. Far from it. And to prove my point I'll let you in on one of the parental-control techniques that I always like to throw in just when me and the auld enemy seem to have entered an extended period of rapprochement. I speak, of course, of the Prolonged Intermittent Nocturnal Wah.

As the name suggests it's a technique that struts, preens and holds court in the Land of Nod. My personal preference is to deploy the opening salvo to coincide with the moment that Hairy and Smooth have finally got to sleep. Then you hit them with a Rising-Wail-And-Shriek. The Wail sets the whole thing in motion; the Shriek lets the parents know it's going to be a long night. That's part of the beauty of the PINW; once you've used it a couple of times the parents get to recognise the signals and know what's coming. It kind of adds to the agony.

Anyway, you've got their attention with the Rising-Wail-And-Shriek so Smooth or Hairy have joined you in your room. (I have noticed it's normally Smooth who turns up. I've no idea why, but think it may have something to do with the inequitable division of power and labour within what is still largely a traditionalist and, some would say, oppressive social engineering unit that plys its trade under the deceptively user friendly title of 'The Family'. Or it could just be that Hairies are lazy.)

So what's your next move?

In the classical interpretation of this technique what you need to do now is to drop the Wail, and put in a little time with that old standby, sobbing. The secret here is to employ a Diminishing Sob that ends in an Air-Gulp-And-Sigh. The purpose is to lull your opponent into a false sense of security. This isn't as easy as it sounds as both Smooth and Hairy are fairly suspicious individuals. That's why before you ever attempt to use this technique you will have to be conversant and confident in that most useful of deceptions – False Sleepy Breathing. Even the most cynical and conspiracy-theory-minded of parents will eventually be taken in by FSB. That's because like so many of the tactics used by the leading confidence tricksters of history (and yes I am including politicians in that group) it dupes your chosen target by telling them precisely what they want to hear. Smooth, having dragged herself from her bed to be by yours really wants to believe you've gone back to sleep. So

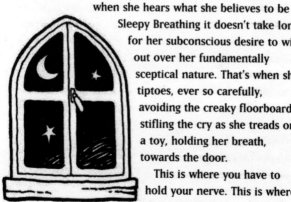

when she hears what she believes to be Sleepy Breathing it doesn't take long for her subconscious desire to win out over her fundamentally sceptical nature. That's when she tiptoes, ever so carefully, avoiding the creaky floorboard, stifling the cry as she treads on a toy, holding her breath, towards the door.

This is where you have to hold your nerve. This is where

you have to keep the rising excitement out of your False Sleepy Breathing. This is where, in the parlance of a slightly different conflict, you have to hold your fire until you see the whites of their eyes. Or in this case, until you hear the hand on the door-handle. Then you let rip. With both barrels. At close range. With the Wah. The mighty Wah.

Smooth won't stand a chance. It's like shooting a fish in a barrel. Smooth, hand on handle, has no other option than to return to your cotside and recommence the whole soothing process.

Your response is obvious. You repeat your actions. Over and over and over again. Of course, you can throw in the odd variation just to keep things interesting. For instance, sometimes let Smooth get out of the door and a few paces down the corridor. Or, and this is my own personal favourite, let Smooth get out of the door, down the corridor, back into bed, all nice and warm and comfy, and just on the very verge of the welcoming balm of sleep, then let rip.

The aim in all this is to keep the show up and running until you notice the first light of morning creeping in under the curtains at your window. When this happens, that's your cue to crash out and slumber. And try to slumber as peacefully and cutely as possible. And for as long as possible. The longer you sleep into the morning, the more worried your totally demoralised, defeated and dejected opponent will be that not only have you wrecked the previous night's sleeping pattern, but also the sleeping pattern of the night to come.

So, do you honestly still think I'm going soft?

# A Brief Observation That I See As A Metaphor For So Much In This Life. It's A Metaphor For How Things That Are At First A Joy, Can, Over The Course Of Time, Or When We Enquire A Little Further, Reveal Themselves To Have A Baser, Maybe Even Distasteful Side

The bottom of the ball pond always smells of wee.

# In Which The Personal Pronoun
# Is No Longer Enough

The thought that stuck in my head, like a half-chewed sweet in the belly button fluff of life, after the incident in the supermarket was 'I am totally responsible for Smooth'. Why the thought hadn't come to me sooner I can't really say. It is blindingly obvious that Smooth, and indeed Hairy, are both dependent upon me for everything. Without me how on earth would they get by? Who would look after them?

I suppose what I'm getting at is that now I had dependants it was abundantly clear that the word 'I' was no longer enough to describe who 'I' was.

Until now I had thought, to misquote Bryan Adams, 'Everything I do, I do it for me.' Now, whereas I wouldn't go so far to as to say that, subsequent to my moment of revelation, I found myself living up to Mr Adams's actual song title, i.e. 'Everything I do, I do it for you', my position had become more 'Everything I do, I do it for us, or more correctly I do loads of things for you and not nearly so many things as I used to do for me'. Bizarrely it felt good. Very good.

Why should this be? Surely being lumbered with dependants is a bind, a drag, a most awful imposition. In many ways, it was. But in others, it gave me a centre, perhaps a purpose, that hadn't been there before.

Having said that having dependants felt, deep down,

inexplicably, good, I have to admit that fairly often, on the surface at least, it was a right pain in the arse. I mean, you wake up in the morning and before you've even had time to wipe the sleep from the corners of your eyes you're engulfed by that god-awful sinking feeling as you try and figure out what the hell you're going to do with the little blighters all day.

# What The Hell To Do With
# The Little Blighters All Day

What follows is a simple schematic I created to divide up the day into manageable chunks. The secret, I soon discovered, was not to think of that vast, empty, yawning abyss of time between waking and sleeping as a single entity, but to split it into segments from the Waking To Breakfast bit through to the After Dinner To Night-Night bit. With this approach, the need to find things for Hairy and Smooth to do all day isn't quite such a daunting prospect.

What follows is just one example of how to construct a matrix of activities so that Hairy and Smooth are constructively (and safely) occupied during the course of the day.

## The Waking To Breakfast Bit

Start by making sure that they're alright. As you are confined to your cot, the way to do this is to summon them with a cheery greeting. Sometimes a cheery greeting isn't enough. Sometimes you greet cheerily for all your worth and no one turns up. Naturally you start to worry. Your call gets just a touch frantic. If there's still no response you find yourself gripped by fear for their safety and end up bawling

your lungs out. This usually works. Indeed, it could be argued that in order to avoid stress on your part, it's best to skip the cheery greeting bit and kick things off with the bawling your lungs out bit. I leave that up to you. It does save time.

Another tactic I sometimes employ is to start the day much earlier than normal. This involves getting up well ahead of my usual time and indulging in a spot of bawling. To my way of thinking it shows commitment; it shows that you really care about Hairy and Smooth and want them to have plenty of time to do things that day. And I'm sure Hairy and Smooth appreciate it. It's just that so early in the morning they are, bless them, not that good at showing their gratitude.

Now Smooth's in the room with you, what next? Well your options at this juncture are the three Cs: Cry, Cuddle or Clamber. They are fairly self-explanatory and I myself favour the Cry, as usually this goes on to incorporate a Cuddle. Cuddling at this early stage in the day is always a big hit. My own theory as to why this should be is that by cuddling, the cuddler (in this case me), reassures the cuddlee (in this case Smooth), that everything is okay at that point in the day when they are at their most confused and vulnerable having not quite completely staggered across the rickety bridge that separates sleep from waking.

About now, Smooth's eyelids may start to droop. On no account let this go any further. If Smooth nods off now it will completely screw up your plans for the rest of the day. So you have to come up with some physical activity that she can get involved in, so that all thoughts of sleep disappear. I suggest that you suggest milk. Put it to her that it would be such fun if she were to take you down to the kitchen, get the milk out of the fridge, put the milk in a bottle, put the bottle in the microwave, then give you the bottle of warmed-up milk to drink. If this all sounds like a lot to explain given your limited actual vocabulary, you can shorthand the whole set of instructions by judicious use of the word 'wah'.

There is, unfortunately, a downside. You have to drink the milk. Even if you don't want to. But I think it's a small sacrifice to get Smooth up and active at the start of the day.

After the milk business, I like to distract Smooth with a bout of playing. However it needs to be carefully selected playing because parents, for some obscure reason, often aren't particularly interested in toys. You can have a whole toy cupboard stuffed with the things and they show not the slightest bit of interest in any of them. So it's pointless getting the toys out. Indeed, in some ways I'm of the opinion that most of the toys are a total waste of money. What appears to be endlessly fascinating to parents, and what they seem to get most excited about, are the things that aren't toys. Such as glasses, and bottles of cleaning fluids, and cutlery (especially knives). Start playing with any of these and like a shot the parents will be up, active and involved. That's why my favourite early morning game that's guaranteed to excite and occupy the parents is 'Getting

Things Out Of Cupboards'. The rules are simple. You get things out of cupboards, then Hairy or Smooth has to put them back. I know it doesn't sound that riveting, but the parents love it. They can play it all day. Indeed so involved do they get in the game that they can even reach the stage where tempers start to fray. Now that's what I call commitment. Sometimes, when H or S are at their most lethargic, you may have to change the game slightly to 'Getting Knives Out Of Drawers'. If this fails, you'll have to resort to a marvellous pastime I've come up with that I call 'Plug Fun'. That always works. That always gets their attention.

Which brings us to breakfast. Breakfast, or indeed any mealtime, should be seen as an ideal opportunity to occupy the parents. It's rather like the food scenario on an airline flight. Most of the time, as a passenger, you're not really hungry, but all that messing about with trolleys and trays and 'fish or chicken?' gives the stewardesses something to do and helps stop them getting bored.

## The After Breakfast To Lunch Bit

The fun really starts after breakfast. You're awake, you've

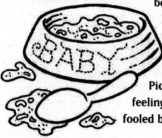

been fed so your blood sugar level is gearing up for action, and the day stretches before you like a blank canvas before Picasso. No doubt Smooth is feeling the same. So don't be fooled by any signs of tiredness she may exhibit — she's raring to go. I think it is important at this point to inject a soupçon of something into the morning that will give Smooth pause for thought and enable her to ponder the fact that life, replete with the possibilities of unalloyed joy though it is, also has a somewhat baser aspect. That's why it's around about now that I usually have a poo. To my way of thinking, there is no better momento mori than a freshly-filled nappy. Especially if you can work in a bit of sideways leakage too.

If when she comes to the actual nappy-changing ritual, Smooth appears to be taking it all in a far too frivolous, even carefree, frame of mind, then I always like to ginger things up by being 'unco-operative'. That soon concentrates her mind on the task in hand.

Post nappy change, a spot more playing is usually a safe bet. By now Smooth may be starting to get cabin fever. When they get like that, the only thing to do is to get them out of the house and let them have a good old run around down the park. Often this involves a change of clothes. Once again the whole clothes-hanging situation affords the astute individual plenty of opportunities to divert and occupy the attention of a bored parent.

When you make it to the park all manner of possibilities abound. Indeed they abound so bountifully that I'll merely list a few for your consideration:

# A list of possibilities that abound in the park

Swings
Slides
Sandpits
Doggies
Puddles
Doggie's poo
Mud
Climbing up things
Falling off things
Ice cream
Bicycles
Running about
Quack-quacks
Chasing quack-quacks
Being chased by quack-quacks
Picking flowers
Hiding

There's much else besides, but you get the picture. The only problem is that parents are irredeemably lazy. Left to their own devices they won't get involved with any of these activities, they won't take advantage of any of these opportunities, they'll just sit around reading a book or a magazine or doing absolutely nothing. It's vital that you lead the way. Yes, I know it's tiring, but if you don't get involved, neither will they.

After the park, when you head home, the parents invariably tend to get a bit cranky. Anything you suggest, and no matter how loudly or frequently you suggest it, they will kick up a fuss. The best thing to do when you do get home is to give them some time and space to calm down by going off and having a nap.

When you wake up after your nap you will undoubtedly find Smooth or Hairy in a much better mood. It's remarkable how the simple 'time-out' technique of a nap can transform even the most cranky, whinging and irritating of parents into paragons of virtue.

Next up is lunch. Treat as breakfast. You'll get away with it because they're easily pleased. But it occurred to me that if I was to map out a whole day for you and suggest that any such plan you make can be adhered to, then I am doing you a considerable disservice. That's because the bitter truth is that with critters like parents you, frankly, can't plan everything. No matter how well you organise, they'll always come up with something that means you have to chuck all your plans out of the buggy. That's because even though they seem to respond so well to regular routines, they seem to like nothing better than occasionally breaking them. And deeply annoying though this is, in another way it is quite heartening and probably vital for their development. If parents were totally happy with everything you organised for them, what prospect do they have of becoming individuals in their own right?

Paradoxically, the hardest part of being totally responsible for your parents is being responsible enough to know that sometimes you have to let them take responsibility for themselves.

# How Deconstructing Language
# Can Often Reveal The Truth

Diarrhoea?
May I suggest that 'dire rear' would be a far more appropriate spelling.

# MONTH XXIII

Nappy or not nappy.
(Don't worry – it'll make sense later.)

# About Time

I've been trying to get to grips with time. You can't see it, you can't taste it, you can't touch it and you can't smell it. You can, however, under certain circumstances, hear it. On those occasions time makes a rhythmic ticking sound interspersed with an equally rhythmic tocking sound. The two sounds exist in a perfectly balanced, symbiotic relationship of equality. Which came first, the tick or the tock, I don't really know, but verbal evidence seems to favour the idea that the tick was the original, with the tock following swiftly on its heels. What is noticeable is that the sound of time tends to have its habitat in the environs of clocks. It's almost as if the clock is like a waterhole on the plains of Africa and that time has gathered there to sup. Move away from the clock and spotting time is like trying to find a well-camouflaged beast in the bush.

How do we really know time exists? It may be largely elusive and ephemeral, but it does leave a trail. You just have to know what to look for. The key is to discern the accumulation of things that happen at fairly regular intervals.

Let me relate this to the world of nappies. You know how when you fill your nappy it gets taken off, wrapped up, and a new one gets put on? Well that is an event that happens at a particular moment in time. Later on in that day it will happen again. And here's the rub, the interval between the first nappy and the second nappy is an amount of time that has passed. So the time itself has gone, but the evidence of its passing exists in the very real, very tangible form of the two full nappies. If you go into your room and three nappies lie neatly wrapped in nappy sacks on the floor, then more time has passed than if you found only two nappy sacks lying there. What I'm saying is that to the discerning eye there is physical evidence to be found that can be thought of as describing the passage of time.

And it's not just nappy sacks. There are the ridges at the corner of Hairy's eyes when he smiles. I gently run my fingers over them and somehow know that much time has passed in front of his face. I touch the corner of my own eyes when I smile and there's nothing there but smooth skin. But such is life. Then my fingers slip and I poke myself in the eye. Which kind of spoils the mood.

# In Which I Try To Make Sense Of The Past, The Present And The Future. But Probably Fail

I'd like to share a few more thoughts on time with you. Time seems to be split up into three distinct components. First there is the present. The present is a moment that exists, momentarily, then is gone. The minute you try to pin it down, it disappears. Paradoxically, it is only elusive if you try to capture it, because if you don't try to trap it you find that you're always in it. Odd.

Next there is the past. The past is the present nudged beyond its use-by date. The past had its moment in the sun of being the present, but has now retired from the fray and has got it's feet up in the garden. If you can imagine the past as a toy cupboard, then memories are the toys you've stacked away in it. The new toys are at the front and you get them out and play with them a lot. The old toys are at the back but you know they're there if you need them. Then behind the old toys are the remnants of broken toys that you never ever get out, but for some reason you can't get rid off. Then there is the future. The future is a toy cupboard with nothing in. Nothing except possibilities.

So what does that make the present? Well, the present is the actual moment you're playing with the toy. This is what life's all about. Dreaming about possible toys is nice, and remembering toys you've played with is good too, but nothing beats actually playing with the toy.

I'll stop there. My head's starting to hurt.

# Sometimes I Do Things And Am So Wrapped Up In What I Am Doing That The Rest Of The World And Everything In It Fades Into Insignificance But Later On When I Look Back On What It Was That Engrossed Me I Have No Idea Why I Found It So Fascinating

I spent most of this morning running naked around a coffee table.

# In The Beginning Was The Word

It is a truth universally acknowledged that first words can be very important. Choose the right ones and what you say will live on in history. Choose the wrong ones and you can kiss posterity goodbye. Who could forget the elegant understatement of 'Dr Livingstone, I presume'? Or the total glorious majesty of 'I'll tell you what I want, what I really, really want'? That's why the selection of the first words you're going to use to communicate to Hairy and Smooth in their own language warrants a serious slab of soul searching.

What I'm talking about here is not the very first, one-off, words that you occasionally utter, but the first coherent, constructed sentence of two or more words. One-off words like 'dada' or 'juice' or 'shoe' (well, I thought I'd show willing) are all well and good, but in truth are little more than crumbs you throw from the table to keep the parents happily clucking over you like a couple of demented chickens. Use one-off words every now and again and, while they get all enthused about your ever-expanding vocabulary, you can usually sneak off and get up to some serious mischief. If you have already indulged in mischief and are awaiting the rebuke you know is heading your way, you can often side-track Hairy or Smooth by pointing at an object you've never identified before and uttering its name. So excited does H or S get that they totally forget your misdemeanour.

For example, if you've managed to open one of the cupboards in the kitchen despite the child-proof locks and found the box with the Bran Flakes in it and opened the box and taken the clip off the bag inside and tipped all the contents all over the kitchen floor and then run up and down on them for a while so that the Bran Flakes get reduced down to what is little more than Bran Bits or even Bran Crumbs and then Smooth turns up and is just about to launch into full-on telling off style scenario, you might be able to distract her by pointing to the window and saying 'condensation'.

This one-off word play, useful though it is, is not what I'm going on about here. What I'm going on about here is an honest to goodness, no nonsense, take no prisoners, sentence. What you're aiming for is a sentence that can be remembered for years to come and be the foundation stone of your legend in the annals of your family's history. I strongly advise you against any sentence that includes the word 'poo'. Other words to be avoided include 'yuk', 'banana', 'Tinky-Winky', 'wee', 'bottom' and 'moussaka'. ( 'Moussaka' might strike you as an odd word to boycott in the circumstances, but in all of history there have been no sentences of any true importance that had the word 'moussaka' in them. Err on the side of caution).

Try and use words that suggest that there's more to you than meets the eye. I've listed a few you might like to consider.

## Ten Useful Words And Phrases For That All Important First Sentence

1. Paradigm 2. Hinterland 3. Ensconce 4. Custard
5. Marsupial 6. Aspiration 7. M.D.F.
8. E-commerce 9. Overlapping wingbacks 10. Festoon

Another useful tactic is to utter your first sentence only when either Hairy or Smooth is present, not when they are both in attendance. When the missing parent turns up and the parent that was there all along tries to get you to repeat what you said, play dumb. This generates all kinds of consternation and ensures that what it is that you said gets repeated over and over and over until it is firmly lodged in both parents' minds.

As an alternative ploy you could always turn to quotation as an apposite way of first crossing this particular bridge of communication. My own personal favourite in these circumstances is this gem from W.C. Fields:

'On the whole, I'd rather be in Philadelphia.'

( N.B. If you are, in fact, already in Philadelphia this quote takes on an altogether more surreal, but not necessarily unpleasing, demeanour.)

It's actually far better if you make up your own first sentence. Who really wants to be remembered for mouthing someone else's words? (Apart from actors and politicians.) So my final advice is consider where you are, consider who you're with and consider how you want to be thought of in the long run. Then go for it.

You're probably wondering what my first words were sentence-wise. Before I spill the beans, let me set the scene. It was a bright sunny morning. Hairy had left early (as he always does). Smooth was just about to take me out for a walk. The doorbell rang and Smooth opened it to find the postman waiting with a package. As the two of them talked I pulled at Smooth's sleeve. When she looked down I hit her with the line I'd been saving up for several weeks.

'I don't think those shoes go with that skirt.'

Well, it made me laugh.

# Be Warned. It's Not Just The Truth That's Out There

There's more stuff I need to tell you about communication. It's not good stuff, but it's important. The problem is this: your parents are better at speaking in their own tongue than you. Of course, this is hardly surprising, but it's a fact that's all to easy to lose sight of as you get swept up in the general euphoria of stockpiling new words and constructing ever more complex sentences.

Although you are patently more intelligent than your parents, because they are more experienced verbally than you, they can often bamboozle you with a flim-flammery of pyrotechnic word-play. So beware. It's all too easy to end up like an unsuspecting tourist catching a taxi in a foreign country. In other words your parents will show no qualms about taking you for a ride.

On occasion they will be, to put it politely, economical with the truth. Or, to put it less politely, they will lie to you. Now a lie is a very interesting and potentially useful concept. It is a purposeful misrepresentation of reality not due to incompetence or ignorance, but due to the deliberate desire of the individual speaking to mislead you for their own often unspecified purposes. When I first encountered a lie, I was completely thrown. Admittedly I was a lot younger than I am now. And I was a lot more gullible.

The first lie was uttered by Smooth. The act was

perpetrated in the setting of so many of the formative
experiences of my early months - the high chair. The words
Smooth used are forever seared on my memory. She said,
and I quote verbatim,

'Tastes nice.'

Well, it didn't. But when I let the offending taupe and
puce-hued gloop dribble from my lips, Smooth repeated
and elaborated upon her calumny.

'Tastes nice! Mmmmmm!'

It still didn't taste nice. But as I hadn't exactly been shown
a menu and a wine list and asked to select for myself what
combination of dishes I thought might amuse my palate that
particular evening, I figured this was all I was going to get
so I might as well bite the bullet and force the stuff down.
So I did. At which point Smooth couldn't resist over-icing
her cake with this particular cold collation of words:

'Mmmmm! See I told you it tastes nice!'

And that was my very first run in with a lie. When I
understood what was going on, I was shocked. It's one thing
to realise and come to terms with the fact that your parents
aren't the brightest nightlights in the house, but it's quite
another thing to face the fact that the devious little urchins
have no qualms about deliberately lying to you. If your
parents, who for some bizarre reason seem to be your fairly
constant travelling companions in the journey of life, can lie
to you, then what hope is there for honesty from anyone
else you ever encounter?

As your own verbal dexterity increases you will be
tempted to try a spot of lying for yourself. You're far better
off to wait until you're older. The problem lies in the fact

that once you venture into the field of wordplay you are immediately at a disadvantage because, frankly, it's your parent's pitch and it's their ball too. I speak from bitter personal experience.

Once I had a few fledgling sentences under my belt I got carried away with the thrill of it all and thought I could take on the parents at the old lying game. So I did. I chose as the location for my first lie a venue that I thought would add a touch of poetic justice to the verbal rematch between myself and Smooth. As I sat in the high chair and innocently ate first one, then another, of the spoons of pale yellow sludge that Smooth unsuspectingly offered, I savoured the moment knowing that I was only seconds away from victory. My lie sat in my head waiting like a finely tuned Ferrari in pole position on the grid at Imola. Then the metaphorical light in my head switched from red to green and I pushed the pedal all the way to the floor. I unleashed the lie.

'All gone.' I said, referring to the sludge.

I waited for an instant to let the full implication of my words reverberate around the insides of Smooth's head. Then I started climbing out of the chair. Mealtime was over. The fat lady had sung. Elvis had most definitely left the building. This lying malarkey was dead easy. Boy was I going to have fun with it in the years ahead.

That's when it happened. That's when the doves of my victory flew straight into the shatter-proof plate glass window of reality and fell, twitching, to the ground.

'No,' said Smooth, 'not all gone. Look.' She

pointed with the spoon at the mountain of dirty yellow sludge still left in the bowl.

It was obviously harder than it appeared. Talk about egg on face. And on bib. And on sleeve. And on leg. And in hair. As the last of the food was shovelled into my dejected mouth Smooth smiled at me and said, just an iota too casually for my liking,

'There, didn't that taste nice!'

# The Joy Of Socks

There will always be a soft spot in my heart for socks. That's because, generally speaking, clothes are possibly the most dispiriting items you encounter in every day life. Whereas run ins with other objects and items throughout the day and night are invariably intermittent, clothes are with you almost all the time. Even when you're fast asleep you're wrapped up in clothes. And throughout the day you are dressed in a constantly changing succession of outfits. Therein lies the problem. You are 'dressed'. You don't do the 'dressing'. Clothes are, in effect, a constant reminder of your powerlessness. Is it any wonder that I so often resist the putting on of clothes by Hairy or Smooth? I see the resistance as nothing more than a totally understandable attempt by the individual to express disapproval at the crude invasion of personal space and unthinking imposition of another's values and taste that is 'dressing'.

Naturally, any reasonably intelligent individual will try to rectify the situation by learning to dress themselves. After all, if Hairy and Smooth can do it, how difficult can it be? Very difficult. Many a frustrating hour I've spent getting both my legs into one leg of my trousers only to discover that, while this may be a most economical arrangement, it is by no means ideal when it comes to the mobility side of things.

Or then there's the Sweatshirt Situation. I mean, getting your head into the sweatshirt is relatively easy, but once inside it's a completely different picture. Or it would be except it's dark in there. Very dark. And as you grope around trying to find the exit you soon discover you've got three choices. Believe me, in the dark as you grapple with indecision and just a little panic, it's very easy to get confused and make the wrong choice.

All of which only leads you to stockpile further negative feelings towards clothes. Indeed, clothes can be interpreted as the ever-present reminders of an individual's lack of empowerment. But every Pandora's Box has to have a little hope in the bottom of it. And in the hostile world of clothes, hope is sock shaped.

Socks come off easily. Socks go on easily. That's why I, and so many of my colleagues, delight in the whole sock thing. We take them off and put them on because we can. It may not be as dramatic a gesture as the burning of bras, or the clenched fist salute at the Mexico Olympics, but to me and my people the removal of the sock is a gesture replete with meaning and power.

# The Stairgate Débacle

^

The path to empowerment is long and winding. And quite hilly in places. (There are also several interesting-looking puddles en route that have to be investigated and generally splashed around in.) But it is, in many ways, the path I have been treading for these past few months, whose highs and lows (and puddles) I have been sharing with you in this journal.

Whereas the first year of my life was pretty much having things done for, and more pertinently, to me, this year has been very much more about doing things for myself. Or, perhaps more accurately, learning to do things for myself. While I have been busy exploring and examining the environments I have found myself in, I have also been assiduously discovering ways in which I can affect these environments.

Moments like that when I discovered I could access whole new green field sites of stuff by the relatively simple act of standing on a chair become key turning points in the developing narrative that is my life. It didn't take me long to figure out that I could move the chair around before standing on it to further increase my sphere of influence, which only goes to show that empowerment is at times like a snowball rolling down a hill gaining mass and momentum as it goes. (Here, I think it only fair to point out a small faux pas on my part. For a short period after the 'standing on a chair' revelation, I laboured under the misapprehension that

I could move the chair to another location after I had stood on it. At the time it seemed to make sense. My mistake was explained to me by that most patient and persistent of teachers – the floor.)

Sometimes, however, the tumbling snowball of empowerment hits a divot in the ground and spins off in the wrong direction, encounters a tree and crumbles into 14¹/₂ pieces. (I know, I've counted.)

The stairgate is a cunning device that stops you gaining access to that most powerful of household objects, the stairs. Stairs comprise a series of tiny bits of floor. Indeed, each bit of floor is so tiny that, for all practical purposes, it is completely useless. There is just about enough room on each stair for two people to stand on. So, take each stair in isolation, and you're looking at a pretty pointless arrangement of space. However, and here is revealed the true genius of the stairs, no stair exists in isolation. You see, just above and just below each stair is another stair. And above and below each of these adjacent stairs is yet another stair. And so on. What this means is that you have a succession of bits of floor that go up, in easily negotiable ascents in one direction, and down, in easily negotiable descents, in the other direction. All of which is incredibly handy as my bedroom is upstairs.

What the stairs do, is that when you are upstairs they enable you to go downstairs, and when you are downstairs they enable you to go upstairs. Or they would, except for one thing. The stairgate. Which is why, amongst my people, the stairgate is a kind of Berlin Wall. And which is why much time, effort and energy is periodically expended in trying to outwit the hated thing.

At the start of the year I favoured the brute force approach. I would stand on the bottom stair, take the stairgate in both hands, and shake it for all I was worth. The obvious flaw was that I, being little more than one year old, wasn't worth that much shaking-wise. Shouting at it didn't help much either, though it did provide an outlet for my pent-up frustrations. After several months unsuccessfully following this purely physical approach to the problem I decided to step back from the frontline of the conflict and observe for a while.

What was revealed was a revelation. Whenever Hairy or Smooth wanted to gain access to the stairs, they didn't take the stairgate on in a crude power struggle, they just fiddled about with something and the stairgate opened up like an over-ripe banana. Obviously I had been using the wrong approach. Obviously the fiddling about approach was the way to reap rewards. So for the next few months I engaged in this more cerebral assault. But to no avail. It proved as fruitless a line of attack as my previous endeavours.

Then one day, emboldened by success in another venture (I think I had just figured out how to open the door of the washing machine and liberate the water) I returned to the fray. I made the fateful decision to abandon the fiddling about approach and return to my earlier tactic. I grabbed the stairgate in both hands, I leant forward and pressed my body against the enemy. I centred my being. Then with a sudden jerk I flung myself back with all the force I could muster.

I now see that I had grown bigger and stronger. Gravity

did the rest. As the paint splintered from the wall and I clung on to the cold hard steel of my foe, I felt my body rotate from the vertical, through the perpendicular to the horizontal. I had won.

The euphoria was short-lived. The pain lasted somewhat longer. As I lay there, trapped beneath the stairgate, bemoaning my predicament in no uncertain terms, it came to me that empowerment is a heady brew that needs to be supped cautiously.

# Reasons To Be Cheerful.
# Part Three

Strawberries

Being tickled

Teddy Bear

Splashing in the bath

Hiding

Banging things

Wrapping myself up in the curtains

Running around naked

Flowers

Being cuddled

Refusing to be cuddled

The Great Nappy Cream Tub Incident

Hiding things

Balloons

Bursting Balloons

Puddles

Jumping

Jumping in puddles

Falling asleep in Smooth's arms

Center Parcs

Slides

Doggies

Putting things over my head and pretending I'm in a tent

Putting things in Hairy's tea

Mud

The moment just before you're about to be tickled

Telephones

Sticker time

Scarecrows jumping up

Playing with the video recorder

My rocking horse

Finding a long forgotten crisp

Tick-tocks

Getting two dummies in one mouth

The sky

Cameras

Running away

Being thrown in the air

Undoing lids

The whole nature-nurture debate

Gar-Gar

I'm sure there's lots of stuff that I've forgotten. But you get my point, don't you? Maybe you should make a list for yourself.

# In Which My Preoccupation With The Products Of My Nether Regions Leads Me To Solve One Of The Great Mysteries Of Life

**H**ow do I know that I exist?

On the face of it the question is ludicrous. After all I obviously exist because I am constantly being bombarded by the evidence of my senses. I know that certain things are hard (e.g. doors when you walk into them), certain things are soft (e.g. gloop when it's shovelled into your mouth), and certain things are both hard and soft (e.g. if you throw the gloop at the door).

I also know I exist because I can change the world around me. I can move object 'A' from position 'B' into position '7'. I can pick up a crayon and test its crayoniness by rubbing it enthusiastically up and down the wall.

Then there's the fact that other people tell me that I exist. Indeed, Hairy and Smooth are forever verifying my existence. Admittedly they tend to do this in exhortations that also include the words 'no', 'naughty', 'mustn't do it', 'gently' and 'noooooooooo!' On the face of it, this seems like all they are doing is telling me off, but deconstruct the messages and another facet of it all becomes clear. If I didn't exist, how could they tell me off?

Then there are other times when the evidence suggests that I don't exist. Or at least it feels like I don't exist. A while back Smooth wanted to put me in the bath. Now normally I love being in the bath. Occasionally, however, I hate the bath. And this was one of those times. I think it was because I'd been pondering that day on the fact that our bodies are 97% water. What struck me is that if this was indeed true, and I got into the bath, then when the plug was pulled out would I run out down the plug hole? Or worse still, would 97% of me run out down the plug hole? And if that was the case, which 3% would remain? Anyway, I wasn't overly keen on heading bathwards that day. I think my general screaming, running away and grabbing onto Smooth's face so tightly that my nails left track marks, made my position abundantly clear. Apparently not. Because in no time at all Hairy had joined the fray and I had joined the water. It was as if I, and what I wanted, didn't exist.

What about when I'm asleep? When I'm asleep do I exist? Many of the criteria that define existence when awake simply don't apply when asleep. When I'm asleep I can't actually do anything. (I can occasionally poo, but that's neither here nor there.) When I'm asleep I can't change the world around me. And when I'm asleep I don't know what's going on. But, maybe to compensate for the lack of sensory stimulation, my mind can go into overdrive. Not the whole mind, only a part of it. The logical part of my mind, the part that sorts out the incoming sensations, takes the night off. This leaves the other part of my mind, the part that imagines things, free to frolic about to its heart's content. Hence dreams.

Thinking about dreams takes me down the tree-lined track that leads to the paddock of the imagination. What, exactly, is going on when I imagine something? When I imagine something am I actually creating something that exists? Is the product of my imagination, in some sense, real? And if it isn't real, what exactly is it?

Indeed what if I am just the product of someone else's imagination? What if I am nothing more than an imagined being in someone else's imagined world?

It makes you think, doesn't it.

It was at this point in my philosophical meanderings that I realised my nappy was full. So I bawled out a cry of discomfort. In no time, Smooth was in attendance doing what Smooth does best. And as I lay with my legs in the air and the chilly caress of the wet wipe brought me sharply back into the world of sensation, I wondered if it was ever thus. Were all eternity's great philosophical thinkers forever cut short in their great philosophical thinkings by the harsh physical realities of the world?

Then it occurred to me, in a moment of blinding revelation, that maybe this was the point. That without physical reality there could be no philosophical conjecture. That pure thought, on its own, with no context to set it in, would be meaningless. And this whole revelation seemed to be crystallised in the very real, very fragrant, nappy that I had just filled. Which is how come, as I watched Smooth tie the nappy into a waiting nappy sack, that the answer to the great question came to me.

How do I know I exist?

I stink therefore I am.

# MONTH XXIV

I had hoped to spend the last month of my journal
pondering the vast imponderables of life. Then Christmas
turned up. And I got carried away with the sheer, glorious
lunacy of it all. Sorry.

To quote one of four very wise men,
'So here it is, Merry Christmas, everybody having fun...'

# In Which I Am Perplexed
# By The Christmas Tree Phenomenon

Certain things belong in certain places. That's just the way it is. The Eiffel Tower belongs in Paris. The White House belongs in Washington. The Elgin Marbles belong in Athens. To have any of these things anywhere else just wouldn't make sense. At times I may have believed that such strictures are fundamentally repressive, at odds with our natural yearning for freedom. But, as I've grown older (and maybe wiser), I've realised that without order the world would be a very different and very difficult place. For instance, what would a sandpit be without certain rules of engagement? What would be the point of playing The Game if there was no way of measuring how much you had scored? How would we organise the equitable distribution of wealth, health and happiness without capitalism, the free market and bus lanes on motorways? So order, on the whole, is a good thing. And certain things belong in certain places. For instance, trees. Trees belong outside.

Except at Christmas.

Yes, it shook me too. I mean, there I was one morning happily running up and down the corridor trying to remember whether it was Rigoletto or Canaletto who was the painter, when I pushed my way through the door that leads to the room with the television and was confronted by a tree. I was dumbfounded. Indeed, my dumb had never been more founded. It was a tree. Inside the house.

Why? If one tree could grow inside the house what was to stop other trees growing inside the house? Even a whole forest of trees growing inside the house? And if that happened, where would we live?

The train of thought that I had inadvertently boarded, was rapidly gathering speed. It was clear that I had to do something. So I reached up and pulled the metaphorical communication cord. And, amidst much shrieking of metal brake on metal wheels, said train of thought ground to a halt.

I acted.

The tree clearly was in the wrong place. It was inside when obviously it should be outside. So the thing to do was to take it outside. And that's what I did, or tried to do. The difficulty was the old Big-Small problem. The tree was big and I was small.

I started off by trying to pick the tree up. I grabbed one of the sticky-out bits. This was a mistake as the sticky-out bit was covered in poky bits. The poky bits, true to their nature, poked my hand. I pulled my hand away. I walked round to the other side of the tree and tried again. But the poky bits were ready for me there too. This tree obviously knew that it didn't belong inside, knew that someone would try to eject it.

Well, I wasn't going to stand for that. I'd show this tree who was boss.

As I looked closer at the tree I detected a possible flaw in its defences. Right at the heart of all the poky, sticky-out bits was another, bigger, sticky-up bit. And this bigger, sticky-up bit wasn't covered in poky bits. 'Ah-hah' I thought. It was like that moment in *Star Wars* when the Rebel Alliance discover that they can blow up the Death Star if they can just get to that window Darth Vader left open round the back.

If I have learned anything from the battles I have waged so far it is that at moments like this, when fate hangs in the balance, caution is useless. So, I stiffened the sinews, summoned up the blood and ran full pelt from one side of the room towards the tree.

As I hurtled towards my adversary, I opened my mouth wide and yelled out the war cry I had been developing over many months for just such a moment.

'Oom-Noom-Noomeeyay!!!!!!!!!!!!!!!!!!!!'

The tree didn't know what had hit it. In a split second I was through the sticky-out bits and I had reached the sticky-up bit.

It was at this point that I realised that there was, shall we say, a small glitch in my plan. So carried away had I been with the need to approach my foe with maximum speed and hence maximum momentum, that I had given little or no thought to the matter of deceleration.

There are many possible ways to describe the sound of a falling tree. But I will make do with but a single word. Loud. A falling tree is loud. Very loud. A falling tree combined with a smashing window, is even louder.

It was a turn of events that rather took me by surprise. But at least the tree was out of the house. Or half out. Which was a start.

Unfortunately, Hairy didn't seem to appreciate the merit of what I had achieved.

# Okay, If That's The Deal Why Don't We Put The Sofa In The Garden?

pparently, Christmas trees are supposed to be inside.
Or more correctly, Christmas trees are supposed to be
outside all through the year, then they're allowed to
come inside for Christmas. Why this should be I'm
not really sure. Maybe they're cold. Anyway, none of this
was explained to me. So when I went into the room and
found the tree growing in the middle of it, I would argue
that it was totally understandable that I reacted in the way
that I did. Indeed, it could even be proposed that I showed
a great deal of initiative and courage.

Hairy thought different. I was, as we say in the trade, CTC.
(Confined To Cot). Much wailing ensued. All to no avail.
Admittedly Hairy did stick his head round the door a couple
of times, but my impassioned pleas for release fell upon
deaf ears. Later, Smooth appeared and that's when I finally
got the explanation about Christmas trees. It must have been
after this that I fell asleep.

When I awoke it was the next day and, as is often the
case, the traumas of the previous day were totally forgotten.
Many a time I've marvelled at how something that caused
such concern and consternation on one day, disappears like
a rusk in warm milk by the next. Sometimes this wiping the
slate clean of the troubles of yesterday makes me think that
I'm too easy going, too much of a soft touch, too willing to

forgive and forget. Maybe I should hold on to my grievances for much longer. That way no one will be getting away with anything. But I eventually came to the conclusion that it's far better to let things go. Otherwise your grievances mooch round like a nappy that needs changing. It's far better to move on. We should all live for the moment and live for today.

Which is precisely what I was trying to do when, the day after the Christmas tree debacle, I went back to the fateful room with the full intention of making my peace with said Christmas tree. I was willing to move on. The Christmas tree however, had other ideas.

In the world of professional card players, there is a commonly held belief that if you've won a lot of money from an opponent, it's best to let them win a little of it back before you walk away from the table. Likewise, amongst my people it is widely acknowledged that once you've established your pre-eminence in any particular sandpit it's good practice to let your vanquished opponents have a bit of a play with any sand or equipment you're not actually interested in. It's all about being magnanimous in victory. And it's not just a matter of good manners, it's also a matter of common sense. Nothing is more likely to stiffen your defeated adversary's resolve than having their nose rubbed in their defeat. When you win, it's best to exhibit a little grace.

Unfortunately the Christmas tree did not hold to this view.

It stood, exactly where it had been before, except now it was festooned in a gaudy, vulgar, totally OTT display of tasteless kitschery. It shrieked a piercing, immature, completely tone-deaf and unnecessary cry of 'Look At Me Everybody. I Won. I Won. I Won'. If someone had told me that Don King was the tree's manager I wouldn't have been at all surprised. It was a complete affront. And totally, totally uncalled for.

My initial instinct was to go for the tree again. I know I had lost the first time round. And I know I would probably lose again. And I know that it would almost certainly result in a prolonged period of CTC. But sometimes you've just gotta do what you've gotta do.

It is at times like this that you finally get a grip on your true measure as an individual. You see, it's not how you handle victory that reveals much about the depth of your character, but how you handle defeat. I am not in any way here singing the praises of the virtues of defeat. I, like most people, would far rather win every time. The point is that sometimes you don't, and when that happens how you deal with it is very important. Especially when your opponent insists on crowing about their victory.

If I say so myself, I'm rather proud of how I handled the situation. I walked calmly up to the Christmas tree and looked at it. That's right, I just looked at it. And as I stood there, quietly taking in all that I saw, in a small, but very real way some of the power shifted back to me. As the lights flashed, as the sparkly stringy stuff sparkled stringily, as the little dangly people dangled, a little self respect grew within me. A little pride returned. And all because I hadn't risen to the bait. All because my reasoning mind had taken precedent over my emotional urges.

And that's when my cunning plan formed.

# The Cunning Plan

When no one was looking I would, one by one, take the decorations off the Christmas tree, and hide them.

# A Cunning Plan Thwarted

Apparently the decorations are supposed to stay on the tree. Apparently it's really important. Especially to Hairy and Smooth. They keep grabbing the decorations from me and hanging them back on the tree. Finally, the issue is resolved by Hairy taking all the decorations off the bottom of the tree (where I can reach) and draping them round the top of the tree (where I can't).

Smooth thinks the tree looks stupid. She discusses the issue, loudly, with Hairy. Hairy discusses the issue, loudly, with her. I detect friction in the air. And the cause of it all is the Christmas tree. I let the parents continue their discussions. In the end, they'll figure out who is the real cuckoo in the nest and get rid of the culprit. It'll just take a little time.

I'm patient. I can wait.

# N.B. At Christmas Don't Sit Underneath The Letter Box

I was leaning against the front door, merrily playing Squish The Biscuit, when it happened.

The word 'engulfed' comes to mind. The word 'cascade' comes to mind. And the word 'ouch' comes to mind. Combine these words together, add a few more and you'll get a general idea of the calamity that had occurred.

As a rule, I have nothing against letters. As a rule, rushing for the letters as soon as they hit the mat and, crucially, getting in a fair bit of ripping, tearing and chewing before Hairy or Smooth realises what's going on, is a mildly diverting way to spend some time of a morning. However, being engulfed in a cascade of letters so that you go 'ouch' (several times and quite loud) is not mildly diverting. It's painful. Especially if, when all the letters have splashed over your head, you look up towards the letter box to see what's going on and a second lot of letters pours towards you, including one whose corner pokes you in the eye as it hits your face. That really is very painful.

Is it any wonder that I grab the offending missive and rip it to shreds? At which point Smooth turns up.

As I grow older I've come to realise that so much in this life is down to timing. Had Smooth turned up earlier, she would have witnessed the unprovoked assault perpetrated upon me and would, no doubt, have offered comfort. Had she turned up later, when I had wrought my act of revenge upon the offending letter, I would have been able to hide the evidence under the other letters and, at the very least, bought myself a bit of running away and hiding time.

Of late, I have realised that sometimes when I have done something that I shouldn't have, and evidence of my misdemeanour exists, e.g. the broken bits of a vase that was less bouncy than it looked, it's possible to avoid the whole telling-off scenario by judicious deployment of a couple of techniques. First there is the Hide The Evidence tactic. A quasi-forensic sweeping up of the crime scene for incriminating evidence is followed by the disposing of said evidence behind or under Big Things. The second tactic is the Hide The Perpetrator manoeuvre. This involves removing yourself from the crime scene and hiding your person behind or under Big Things. Unfortunately, the last time I was involved in such escapades I was so carried away by the adrenaline rush of my misdemeanours that I combined the two techniques and hid myself and the evidence in the same place, namely behind the sofa. (You wouldn't have had to be M. Hercule Poirot to figure that one out.)

Timing is everything. When Smooth arrived all she saw was yours truly apparently engaged in an act of uncalled-for hooliganism. Remonstration followed . And a 'scene'. All because I was sitting in the wrong place, namely under the letter box, at the wrong time, namely Christmas. Which brings me to my closing bit of advice and my closing question. Advice: don't sit under the letter box at Christmas. Question: wouldn't it be better, and safer, if the extra letters that turn up at Christmas could somehow be spread throughout the rest of the year?

# In Which I Am Scared By A Badly Dressed Fat Man With An Obviously Fake Beard

So we're out. On a trip. 'We' being me and Smooth. We travel, by bus (whose wheels go round and round, round and round, round and round) to the shops. Smooth is very excited. She tries to communicate her excitement to me, but none of what she says seems to make much sense. We go into a particular shop and join a queue. The queue is made up of colleagues accompanied by their Smooths. One is accompanied by a Hairy. The Smooths chat merrily to each other, but the Hairy keeps himself to himself. It's a pattern of behaviour I have observed time and time again and I have to admit it makes me feel a little sorry for the guy. I must get my Hairy more involved in my life. I don't want him missing out on all the good stuff I get up to. I'm sure that his life when he's away from me can't be anywhere near as interesting or as much fun as it is when he's with me. What on earth can he find to do all day? It's not as if he's that bright. I have this vision of him sitting at a big table all day, playing with bits of paper, and occasionally talking to other people about stuff that isn't very important. But that can't be right, can it? Why would he stick with it?

Anyway, we're in a queue. A queue is a period of waiting organised in a three-dimensional, linear form. You stand behind someone who's standing behind someone and then someone comes and stands behind you. After this has gone on for a while, you observe that the person you're standing behind is no longer standing behind anyone. Then the person you're standing behind leaves and, bizarrely, the queue that was all in front of you at the start, is all behind you now. And then something happens. And that's how a queue works.

My personal theory is that this whole queue thing is just a way to occupy you so that you don't actually notice that all you are doing is waiting. Waiting is an odd concept too. Waiting is all about doing nothing. But waiting has been cunningly hyped as doing nothing with an aim in mind. I can't see the point. If you want to do something, why not just do it? If you can't do the thing you want to do straight away, why not do something else? Standing around in line doing nothing in a queue, is a shocking denial of the myriad possibilities that life holds. I always advise colleagues who find themselves in any queue-style scenarios, to run around and try to instigate a popular uprising against the bourgeois conformity and individuality-crushing social order that is the very core of the queue. To put it into a more populist call-to-arms (and in this case legs) 'Don't just stand there! Do something!'

Anyway, we were in a queue.

All the other Smooths were as excited as mine. The lone Hairy was as well, but had no one to share his excitement with. Much to my surprise some of my bigger colleagues were also excited. One was even jumping up and down in excitement. (N.B. such clichéd behaviour impresses no one. My own favoured way of expressing excitement is to quizzically raise one eyebrow and let the merest hint of a smile gather in the corner of my mouth. A bit like Sean

Connery used to do.) All this excitement made me think that we were in line for something rather special. So, very much against my better judgement, I abandoned the rabble-rousing approach I usually take to all queue situations and decided to wait. Quietly.

You would think that Smooth, who normally has all manner of difficulties to get me to wait quietly in a queue for anything, would be pleased with my restrained demeanour. But no. We were apparently waiting for something very very exciting and so I was supposed to wait in a calm, yet somehow excited fashion. She kept up a running commentary on how far we were up the queue each time someone left the front of it and went through the funny little doorway festooned with glittery white stuff. The closer we got to the front of the queue, the more excited Smooth got. And that's when the truth dawned upon me. This treat was really a treat for Smooth. We were doing it so that she could have a good time. I was merely the cover story. When I looked around at everyone else in the queue the accuracy of my hypothesis was plain to see. In every case, the Smooth (and the lone Hairy) was more excited than the person they had come with.

I was being shamelessly used as a mere means of access to some, as yet, unspecified event that Smooth was longing to participate in! I was all set to leap into action and ferment revolt amongst my people when I discovered that we had reached the front of the queue. I looked up at Smooth and saw that she was so excited about what was to happen that my resolve weakened. How bad could it be? So we went in.

You know how sometimes you go somewhere and you know straight away that something isn't right?

For a start, there was a Christmas tree there. As you know, me and Christmas trees weren't exactly on 'big hug' terms. Then there was The Fat Man. The Fat Man In The Red Suit. The Fat Man In The Red Suit With The Obviously Fake Beard. Red, I had recently discovered, was a colour that in certain circumstances denoted danger. And this deeply dodgy looking character was dressed, head to toe, in the stuff. I was immediately on my guard. Second off, he was a stranger. Strangers, too, are something I have often been warned about. Thirdly, there was the whole fake beard shtick. What was he hiding from? And if he thinks that pathetic attempt at a beard is going to fool anyone, not only is he on the run, but he's also obviously deranged.

I looked towards Smooth to make sure she understood the danger we were clearly in. I looked in a way that I hope would appear casual so as not to alert The Fat Man to my growing concern. To my horror Smooth was oblivious to our predicament. She was smiling. She was smiling at The Fat Man. And then The Fat Man spoke. And this is what he said. And I quote his words exactly.

'Yo Ho Ho! And have you been a good little thing all year?'

What the hell did 'yo ho ho' mean? And why should my behaviour be any concern of yours, you creep, I've only just met you.

I spun away from the horrific apparition and reached my arms up towards Smooth. She picked me up and for one joyous instant I thought we were going to make a fast getaway. But then I saw that she was laughing. Then — and if you are of a nervous disposition, please look away now — she handed me over to The Fat Man and sat me on his lap.

Enough was enough. I had to do something to prove to Smooth that all was not what it seemed. I had to alert her to the danger we were sinking deeper and deeper into. I had to snap her back to her senses. I reached up with both hands, grabbed The Fat Man's Beard, and pulled for all I was worth, screaming at the top of my lungs as I did so. He shrieked and leapt to his feet. I slid to the floor. Smooth bundled me up in her arms, told me off and apologised to The Fat Man. Yes, I kid you not, she told me off and apologised to The Fat Man.

With a struggle The Fat Man retrieved his fake beard from my hands and smiled a smile at my mother that was as false as everything else about him. Then he patted me just a little bit too hard on the head and gave Smooth a small, brightly wrapped package. Smooth accepted the package gratefully and backed out of the room with me in her arms.

As we left the shop we went back past the queue of people. I started shouting warnings at them. But it was no use, the Smooths (and the one Hairy) just looked and smiled at my Smooth indulgently. And as I watched I saw the queue shuffle forward again. Was there to be no end to the horror?

When we got home Smooth gave the package to me. I opened it. Inside was a small, furry hedgehog. Apparently it was a gift. From The Fat Man In The Red Suit With The Obviously Fake Beard who, apparently, trades under the pseudonym of Father Christmas. And it was for me. But I didn't want it. It was crap. And as I lay in bed that night I thought to myself, is this really what Christmas is all about? Does it come down to a lot of stress and hassle and over-hyped expectations that can't be fulfilled and strange people in strange clothes behaving strangely and presents you never really wanted in the first place?

There must be more to it than that?

# Of Course There's More to Christmas Than That. There's Parties

T he word on the streets is that Christmas is, officially, the party season. Who am I to argue with that? I love parties. I love the sights. The sounds. The smells. The tastes. The constant flux of individuals cavorting in a space solely defined by the relaxation of so many of the normal rules of social interaction.

And then there's the Running About. You can run about a lot at a party and no one really seems to mind. Even the usual embargo on shrieking is lifted. You can indulge in all that R A and S work that ordinarily would result in admonition, as long as you don't go over the top. But then, going over the top is such fun.

Being at a party must be similar to what it was like when the Berlin Wall came down. Only the food is better. And there's so much to choose from. AND, and this is a big 'and', in fact it could well be the biggest 'and' in the whole book, AND it's at a sensible height. On a normal day, in a non party scenario, food is invariably positioned on a table that you can't reach.

Now what is the point of that?

If they want you to eat is it too much to ask that they put the food somewhere you can get to it? Of course, you do get to the food, but always on their terms. You have to be lifted up in to a chair and then strapped in before you can eat. Now, on a couple of occasions I tried to climb up and into my chair myself. But that went down like a tower of bricks. Half way through my ascent I would be unceremoniously grabbed, lifted, dumped and strapped in. Only then was I granted access to the food.

At a party, however, it's all different. At a party food can be found not only on the high tables, but also on the low tables. What's more, at a party you're not confronted with the take it or leave it, like it or lump it, no-choice choice of food that you think would have disappeared with the demise of the monolithic, eastern European, communist dictatorships that fell like so many dominoes in the aftermath of the demolition of the Berlin Wall I mentioned earlier. Oh no. At a party there's loads of food to choose from. Including, be still my beating heart, crisps of all shapes, sizes and flavours.

Is it a wonder that I love to party. Indeed, is it any wonder that I love to paaaaarrrrrttty! There can be few thrills as great as to find your self running and shrieking down a strange corridor, diving into a room, and through a forest of legs glimpsing that first, glorious sight of a low level table covered with food. And when you hack your way through the undergrowth of shoes, shins, ankles and knees you discover, oh joy of joys, there's even squidgy food laid out with no one there to stop you from squidging it.

How good can life get?

# The Day Itself

Of course I am editing a lot of stuff out. Christmas seemed to overflow at the seams like a nappy that had been left on far too long. You could hardly go anywhere without running into whole plantations of Christmas trees. Dodgily dressed, badly disguised Fat Men were popping up with alarming regularity. A ludicrous rumour swept through the community that, come the night before Christmas day, one of these characters would actually try a spot of breaking and entering on the old homestead via, believe it or not, the chimney. It is a patently ludicrous idea, but such was the grip of collective Christmas hysteria on my people that several of my older colleagues vowed to stay up all night to protect the home against just such an invasion.

You know how at the end of *Chinatown* someone explains the mayhem that has engulfed Jack Nicholson by saying something along the lines of 'Don't worry about it, it's just Chinatown'. Well, that's how I felt about the madness that had engulfed me. It was just 'Christmas'. No point in trying to make sense of it, no point in trying to change it. The best thing you could do was just survive it. And thank whoever you thank in these circumstances that it only happens once a year.

Don't get me wrong. I'm not saying that Christmas is a complete downer. Indeed I believe that, with a little planning, the exact opposite can be the case. It's just that you have to make sure that you don't fall prey to the hype that surrounds the whole thing. You have to find a meaning that makes sense for you.

All of which brings me to the day itself. Christmas.

That's my first problem with the whole Christmas thing as it is currently celebrated. It's all focused on one, single day. Now how on earth can one day live up to all the expectations. It's just one day. Admittedly you get to stay up later than normal and no one even tried once to put me down for a nap, but it is still just one day. You also get to wear a whole new outfit. And, if I say so myself, I did look kind of chic in the togs that had been chosen for me. The downside is that if you get even one single Marmitey crumb or dribble of juice on it, all hell breaks loose. Apparently the whole point of the new outfit malarkey is so that Hairy and Smooth and their associates can stand around looking at you and go 'Ahhhhh!' Appear in the new outfit accessorised by even the most tastefully understated of Marmite or juice stains and  Smooth looks  at you and goes 'Ohhhhhhh!' If you don't want to be whisked away and redressed just a little too brusquely, it's best to keep the new clobber pristine. Or as pristine as a one year old can keep anything.

Another thing that happens at Christmas is that loads of people turn up and hang around all day waiting to be fed. I have observed that, generally speaking, there are two types of people in the world. There are those who you glimpse fleetingly on your trips outside and never see again. Then there are those who keep recurring, for no apparent reason, and who you see, relatively, often. For this reason I have decided to call this second group of people 'relatives'. And it is these 'relatives' who turn up at Christmas and wait to be fed. The good thing is that while they're waiting to be fed they have very little to do so they pass the time playing with you. It has to be said they aren't, as a rule, very good. But what they lack in skill, they make up for in enthusiasm. Don't be too picky and just accept that you're in for a quantity, not quality play experience.

There will come a point where the relatives' patent lack of playing skills will start to annoy you. Don't let it get to you. Go with the flow. Because at some point in the day something truly remarkable will happen. The relatives will give you presents. And I have this theory that the size of the present they give you is in some way related to the amount you play with them.

Why the relatives should give you presents is anyone's guess. My belief is that the present is the physical expression of a network of kinships, associations and obligations. And it gives you something to play with when the relative in question runs out of steam for your actual, hands-on, playing type behaviour. Also the fact that the present remains with you after the relative has left means that you always possess a symbol of your relationship with said relative.

The etiquette of present acceptance insists that on receiving the gift you exhibit your approval in one of three ways:

1 You jump up and down.
2 You run round and round waving the present in the air.

3 You ignore the present entirely and sit playing with the box that it came in.

For some obscure reason, response 3 is the one that the relatives enjoy most. But not all the relatives. It's only the relatives who didn't give you that particular present who go for the fact that you prefer the box. The actual present giver would much rather you chose response 1 or 2.

But all that is largely a side show. The real point of the whole affair is that you're getting more stuff. Stuff that wasn't yours the day before, is now. And usually most of the stuff you get given is pretty damn funky. However, you just get given so much stuff that it makes you wonder when you will ever have enough time to play with it all. Indeed you might even have to bus in colleagues from elsewhere and get them involved in some serious playing just to make sure that everything does get played with. But why worry about that now? Now all you really need to do is to wallow in the wonder of all the new stuff that heads your way.

Then there's the food. Christmas day is a day crammed full of food. Everywhere you look, food looks back at you. There's more food than you can shake a stick at. I know this for a fact as I tried shaking a stick at all the food. But I couldn't, there was just too much of the stuff. (And anyway Hairy took the stick off me muttering something about a Mont Blanc not being a toy.) Then around lunch time the parents and the relatives play this brilliant game where they all sit around and try to see who can eat the most food. (Hairy won.) Then they all go into the other room, put the television on and play another game where they all see who can snore the loudest. (Hairy won again.) It's during this particular game that you can have the most fun. That's because all the relatives are so intent on the game they're playing, no one really notices what you're up to. Then everyone wakes up and eats more food. Then everyone goes away. And then you go to bed. And when you wake up the next day it's all over.

So that's what Christmas day is like. And I have to say, confusing and overhyped though it is, it is a lot of fun. And you get to keep the presents. Which is nice.

# But What Does It All Mean?

It's a good question. And I'm not sure I have the answer. But I do have a theory. I'm not saying it's the right theory, but it is my theory and I'm rather proud of it. Christmas comes, pretty much, at the end of the year. Obviously, therefore, it is something to do with marking the end of that year. As it is no doubt celebratory in its nature it is, equally obviously, some kind of celebration. Combine the two thoughts and you get the idea that Christmas is a celebration that marks the end of the year. But what precisely is being celebrated?

To answer this question I believe one has to deconstruct the mechanics of the event. Two things seem to be central to the whole Christmas experience. First there are presents. Second there is food. Consider these facts for any length of time and it soon becomes obvious that what links them is that they are both, in one sense or another, to do with consumption.

So that's the heart of my thesis. Christmas is an end-of-the-year celebration of consumption. But why do we need such a celebration at such a time? Maybe it's something to do with the fact that the days get darker sooner now. And the fact that outside is much colder than it used to be. And that Hairy and Smooth and almost everyone else is just a bit grumpier than they used to be when encountered earlier in the year, for example when they were on the beach. And the sun seems much more tired at the moment. It gets up later, is pretty knackered most of the day, and goes to bed much earlier. All of which means that we (and I use the term 'we' here in very much a macro sense, referring to what passes for society as a whole) could all do with a little cheering up. And what better way to cheer someone up than with a celebration? And what better way to cheer up a society than to celebrate the core belief, principle and driving force of that society?

So that's my theory in full. Christmas is an end of the year celebration designed to cheer people up in an otherwise glum time by the glorification of consumption, the key force that drives and holds together the society we live in. Look at it this way and it's clear that Christmas is really for the parents. It's a magical time for them. It's something they can really believe in.

As for me, I can take it or leave it. Getting presents was kind of fun, though. I could get used to that. And it obviously meant a lot to Hairy and Smooth that I liked the presents I was given. Now, if I was of a real cynical bent, I could interpret the parents' behaviour as a way of trying to get me to buy into and believe in society's consumerist value system. But, to be honest, they're not that clever. And, I hope, I have a bit more depth about me than to fall for such a clumsy ploy.

After all, presents are only things. And who wants to live in a society where things are accorded so much importance?

# And Finally, While We're On The Subject Of Christmas Here's A Short Treatise On The Enduring Appeal Of The Ephemeral. (Or Why The Wrapping Paper And The Box Are Always More Interesting Than The Present)

The present will still be there the next day, the wrapping paper and the box won't. Given this arrangement it only seems fair to afford them just a bit of attention while they're still around.

# OUTRODUCTION

Sinatra, when he was taking his leave, used to state his case (of which he was certain). Hamlet reckoned that the rest was silence. And the Teletubbies indulge in a spot of Tubby bye-byes by one by one waving their hands in the air, then jumping into a hole in the ground. I mention all this only because I too am about to bid you a fond farewell, but reckon I should leave you with some profound message.

All I can really hope is that you've enjoyed our time together and have gained just a little insight into what it's like to be a one year old these days. I suppose if I've achieved that, then I've achieved something and this tome can rest contentedly alongside the Rosetta Stone, Leonardo's notebooks, the American Declaration of Independence and the last *Blackadder* script as another document that in time will prove a key turning point in the history of civilisation.

All I'll add is that if you've enjoyed the book do tell your friends. Or better still buy it for them. You see the thing is, I'm about to embark on the old potty training scenario. So I reckon I'm going to need all the royalty cheques I can lay my hands on just to cover the dry cleaning bills.

# THE END